TALK TO YOUR ANGELS

HOW TO HAVE GREAT ANGEL
CONVERSATIONS IN 30 DAYS OR LESS

Catherine Wishart

BALBOA.
PRESS
A DIVISION OF HAY HOUSE

Balboa Press books may be ordered through booksellers or by contacting:

Balboa Press
A Division of Hay House
1663 Liberty Drive
Bloomington, IN 47403
www.balboapress.com
1 (877) 407-4847

Because of the dynamic nature of the Internet, any web addresses or links contained in this book may have changed since publication and may no longer be valid. The views expressed in this work are solely those of the author and do not necessarily reflect the views of the publisher, and the publisher hereby disclaims any responsibility for them.

The author of this book does not dispense medical advice or prescribe the use of any technique as a form of treatment for physical, emotional, or medical problems without the advice of a physician, either directly or indirectly. The intent of the author is only to offer information of a general nature to help you in your quest for emotional and spiritual well-being. In the event you use any of the information in this book for yourself, which is your constitutional right, the author and the publisher assume no responsibility for your actions.

Any people depicted in stock imagery provided by Thinkstock are models, and such images are being used for illustrative purposes only. Certain stock imagery © Thinkstock.

Print information available on the last page.

ISBN: 978-1-5043-7739-3 (sc)
ISBN: 978-1-5043-7740-9 (hc)
ISBN: 978-1-5043-7778-2 (e)

Library of Congress Control Number: 2017904723

Balboa Press rev. date: 04/18/2017

Angels, angels, everywhere

Angels love to help us. Their only requirement for helping you is that you ask them to. Because of the law of free will, Angels cannot step in to help unless you ask first. The only time they have license to break this rule, is if you are in a life-endangering situation before your time to leave this planet.

There are zillions of angels, just as there are zillions of stars, so never worry that you are taking angels away from other people by asking for their help. Plus, angels can be in more than one place at a time. There are lots of bored, unemployed angels waiting to help.

You can ask the angels for help with anything, big things, little things and teensy weensy things. There is no order of miracles in the universe, one miracle is just as easy for divine source to accomplish as another. What may seem like a HUGE miracle for us as humans, for the angels, it may seem as easy as finding you a parking spot.

The angels can help you with everything from finding a new job, discovering your life purpose, attracting love, attracting money, helping you navigate a divorce or break-up, healing from an illness, knocking some sense into you, and locating the remote control for your TV. Whatever you need, the angels love to help.

I asked the angels what their wish for this book is, and this is what they said: "*We want humans to call on us more. We want people to know they are never alone, that there is heavenly help available to them all the time. We want people to know we are real, that they can talk to us, see us, hear us and feel us. We want people to know we love you and will always guide you to the people, places and things that are for your highest good. We want you to know we can guide, help, comfort, protect and assist you. We are helpers from the unseen realms, but we can help you in very concrete, tangible ways. Our wish is this book provides people with a practical way to contact us, and learn the angel language.*"

I hope these techniques change your life as much as they have changed mine.

To my two sons Logan Wishart and Kylan Wishart

The two most beautiful sons in the world

Thank you for your unwavering belief in me

Thank you for buying me a computer ☺

Thank you for our family

Love always

Mom xox

Dec 6th, 2016

ACKNOWLEDGMENTS

No book is written alone, once my words are written they are transformed by the editors, designers and dream team of a publishing company.

Special Thanks to:

Justine Saints, Justine thank you for helping me pick up a pen again and holding my hand on this journey. You are the patron saint of authors.

The past decade, I know it is unusual to thank a decade instead of a person, but much of what you hold in your hands is wisdom gleaned from the past decade. Angels as much as I have complained over the years, I love you and thank you.

Sandy Fabrin, for your restoration of my soul. I thank you.

Nikki Rettford, for your help with my health I appreciate you so much. Huntington Beach, to Lisa, Chelsea, Meghan, Lauren, Carolyn, Christine, Annie, John, and so many more beautiful souls, thank you for welcoming me into your community.

Shani Orona, thank you soul sister, for being you.

Yancey Milloy, for our many psychic conversations and all the years you have helped me I thank you.

Sina, Leigh and your beautiful sons, thank you for all the singing, laughter, healing and for being our "other" Kiwi family.

Jeanette Horomia, thank you so very much for your generosity. Your candles light up my nights.

Sheena, my favorite gypsy dodge sister, thank you for teaching me gypsy history and culture. I love our adventures.

Karim White, for your patience, encouragement and faith, thank you. You continue to inspire me with your dreams, music and our artistic endeavors

Kate La Trobe, thank you for all your encouragement and our skype conversations Chris Penczak, thank you for encouraging me too and for sending me a care package while I was in New Zealand.

My dear brother David, Victoria and my beautiful niece and nephews, Renata, Benicio and Vicente, Aunty and Uncle, and Robyn. Thank you for all your help.

Denise Jones-Tutaki, thank you so much, for editing this book, for being a kick ass friend/sister. Here's to our days at The Chronic.

My Unseen Mentors

Wayne Dyer, I was at your last speech in New Zealand in 2015. You inspired me in my teens when Your Erroneous Zones first came out, and you continue to inspire me today.

Represent and Rephard.com, you guys taught me how to dig deep and "step it up for this one!"

Doreen Virtue, you were my unseen mentor when I wrote Teen Goddess and you continue to inspire me today.

To all my clients, students and YouTube followers over the years, thank you for enriching my life, and teaching me too.

CONTENTS

HOW TO USE THIS BOOK

"I'm sick of having one sided conversations with my angels...when are they going to answer?" asked my friend Lex, and thus this book was born. I realized after twenty-five years of professionally doing angel readings, workshops, life coaching and psychic readings, that even though eighty percent of Americans believe in angels, there is a majority who do not know how to have a meaningful relationship with them.

I can tell you everything in here has been tested by me, repeatedly, and taught to many of my clients. When things are good, it is easy to have faith, but during transition or crisis, it can be scary to have faith. If you are holding this book in your hands, I promise you that you will have deepened your connection with your guardian angel, as well as other angels, by the time you finish this course.

This book is a workbook. I can provide you with the information, but to talk "angel language," you are going to have to practice. To learn a language takes ten hours daily for forty-eight days if it is an easy language, and seventy-two if it is a difficult language. Learning a new language does not happen overnight. I wrote this book in workbook style, so that you can use it daily.

Each day you can work at your own pace to assist your angel journey and discover what has worked for me, the methods I use with my clients, and how you can start your angel connection today. By the end of day one, I promise you will already be on your way to having the most important relationship you can have in life.

Your Guardian Angel is your best friend, your cheerleader, your personal bodyguard. Your Angel Guide helps you to navigate an at times, challenging earthly realm. Within thirty days you will have learned how to: see angels, how to feel them, how to talk to them, how to see, hear and feel other people's angels, how to channel angels, how to find a good reader, as well as meeting The Angel Council of Light and ten different archangels.

This is a fun workbook in bite-size pieces. It is a day-by-day journal of your relationship with angels for you to use, and reuse, as often as you like. When I teach people to talk to their angels, the first step I advise is to buy a notebook and write "My Angel Journey" on the front, and use it every day for at least thirty days to write your angel conversations. Spend twenty minutes every day practicing talking with your angels. Every single day. No exceptions.

What you are holding is your own angel journey, and the techniques I have taught for many years. Make it yours – underline what you like, scribble out what you don't. It is made for you and your relationship with angels.

Love, Catherine.

There are two parts to this book: The first twenty days teach you a new skill each day, like how to see angels, how to feel angels, what is an angel, and other techniques. The book is written so each technique builds upon the day before, so I recommend doing the chapters on a day-by-day basis in the order they are written, because there is a reasoning behind the way I teach you the skills in that order.

Even if it takes you longer than one day to do any given chapter, choose a time now and put it in your phone or day planner. Choose twenty minutes at the same time each day. For example, ninepm. Set your calendar with a reminder for twenty minutes at ninepm for the next thirty days, save it as "My Angel Homework." You are learning a new language. You are learning how to talk to angels and how they will talk back to you. So it is important you do your homework. Daily practice is best – not three-hour cramming sessions on the weekend! At the end of this book you will have created a new habit that you can continue for as long as you want. You will have learned a new language, you may not be fluent in it – but if you keep practicing you will become fluent.

The second part focuses on Ten Days of Archangels, and here you will learn about ten archangels and how they can help you, and about The Angel Council of Light who you can call on for help, and seventy-two angels who all specialize in different areas.

WRITING THIS BOOK

Each book has a life of its own. I am simply the scribe. I listen and I write down what I hear with a combination of my psychic senses, and researched knowledge. While writing this book, I had some health issues, and was mad at the angels. There were many days I doubted their existence. But I continued to talk to them every day anyway. I have been talking to angels since I was three. I can't imagine a day of not talking to them.

As I wrote each chapter, I practiced the techniques to make sure they still worked. Even though most of the time I practice on autopilot, it was good to have the time to practice them deliberately. I have been talking to angels for as long as I can remember, and don't know what it is like to live a life where you don't talk to them. I never cease to be amazed at the miracles they help produce. Angels are divine messengers, emanations of divine source or God, and they will help you with anything. Yesterday I wrote in my angel journal; *"Angels, please find me the perfect place to live. May something wonderful open up where I would want to live within seven days, 'cos I'm freaking out right now."*

This morning when I woke up there was an email from the place I had wanted to live. They had two places available, the email said. So I know these techniques work. And sometimes very quickly. As I wrote about each angel, each chapter took on a life of its own. The angels said: *"We want humans to have more direct experiences with us."* They wrote through me, and I learned more about each angel's personality, and qualities, as I wrote. The angels were beside me while this book was written. They were quite adamant about what they wanted in the book. I am grateful for the opportunity to write this book. It has deepened my own relationship with the angels. Thank you, Angels. Help us all to remember that you always have our back.

DAY ONE. SO, WHAT IS AN ANGEL ANYWAY?

What would you do if an angel walked into the room where you are right now and sat down beside you?

"Hello _____ (your name), he or she says. "I am your guardian angel, and I am here to help you. From now on you don't have to worry about anything, because I will help you take care of everything. From this moment on, you will have all the heavenly assistance you need. And I will always be with you, for now and forever.

"Whenever a problem comes up, I will be right here along with a host of other angels to give you advice. When you need something, I will be here to tell you how to get it. And I will help you with your dreams too. If you trust me and follow my instructions, I will lead you to the right people, places, and opportunities that will bring your dreams to life.

"Plus, when you are having a hard time with someone, I will help you see things from a different perspective, so you can extend yourself in compassion, and not feel so hurt by others' actions. And, I am going to help take away your pain and fear, and replace it with joy and love. I will also comfort you when you ask.

"From now on, you and me, we're a team. All the angelic assistance you need is right here beside you, and all you have to do to activate it is just ask."

What would you do if that happened?

Angel Workout

Throughout this book, you will see lots of angel workouts. This is your angel homework, think of them as soul stretches that you practice daily.

The point is you already have a guardian angel. And you have a whole team of angels' who are on your side, willing to champion your dreams for you and help you with life's challenges. Your angels surround you right now. There is an angel right beside you, hovering behind your left shoulder. This is your guardian angel, and he or she never leaves your side. There are many other angels with you right now, and they all want to talk to you.

As you go through your day, you will pass by many more angels. There are angels in the shopping mall riding up and down the escalators, there are angels in school halls perched up on the locker doors, there are angels in the grocery store whispering gentle nudges to you to make healthy choices for your purchases. There are angels on earth walking amongst us. Whether you can see angels or not does not matter – they are there anyway and it is quite likely that you 'bump' into different angels' several times each day. There are literally billions of angels on earth and they are all sent here to help, guide, protect and comfort you.

Angel Workout

Close your eyes and imagine the above scenario is taking place. Your angel walks into the room and sits down beside you and tells you all the angelic assistance you need is available to you right now.

What one question would you ask your angel?

What one situation would you want help with today?

What is one thing you would like the angels to help you with this week?

What's your favorite angel story?

Everybody has at least one angel story, whether it happened to you, or someone else. By telling our angel stories and hearing others' stories, we come to see how much the angels are involved in daily life.

Write about your angel story here.

My Angel Story (this really happened too!)

What are Angels?

According to my dictionary, an angel is:

- ♥ One of a class of spiritual beings which attend to God.
- ♥ A divine messenger from God.
- ♥ A typically benevolent celestial being that acts as an intermediary between heaven and earth, especially in Christianity, Judaism, Islam, and Zoroastrianism.
- ♥ A representation of such a being, especially in Christianity, conventionally in the image of a human figure with a halo and wings.
- ♥ Angels Christianity: The last of the nine orders of angels in medieval angelology. From the highest to the lowest in rank, the orders are: seraphim, cherubim, thrones, dominations or dominions, virtues, powers, principalities, archangels, and angels.
- ♥ A guardian spirit or guiding influence.
- ♥ a. A kind and lovable person. b. One who manifests goodness, purity, and selflessness. [Middle English, from Old English engel, or Old French Angele, both from Late Latin angelus, from Late Greek angelos, from Greek, messenger]. An intercessor between humans and God.

I believe angels are spiritual beings. They vibrate at a higher frequency than humans. therefore it is harder to see them. Angels are a species of the angelic race, just as humans are a species of the human race. Within the angelic race are many kinds of angels which you will learn about.

The dominions, the powers, the virtues are all different races within the angel realm. Think of them like families. The angel family has Gabriel as the manager or supervising angel.

People experience angel's energy as feminine or masculine, although angels are genderless. For example, Chamuel always shows up as a female to me, as does Gabriel, to some people their energy may feel more masculine. I experience her as female so I see Chamuel as the queen angel of the Seraphim family. Some people think of Chamuel as masculine energy so could think of him as the King or commander of the Seraphim family and Gabriel as the king of the angels.

Michael always shows up as male to me, he is the angel of the heart, and the King of the Power family, although some traditions say he is the King of the Virtue family depending on which tradition you follow. Don't worry if this seems like a lot of information. Know that you will learn more about the nine angel groups or family's in the last ten days. Thinking of them as families rather than "choirs" can make the angels feel more accessible.

Angels act as bridges between the spirit world of heaven, and the concrete manifest world of earth. One of their greatest function's is to help humans manifest their desires from the spirit world of ideas and imagination, into the physical world of reality.

Angels are here to love, comfort and assist us. They teach us how to apply spiritual principles in our daily lives. They teach us how to love others. They bring us messages from beings in the spirit world, from God, the Goddess or from Mother Mary, and other ascended masters like Jesus, Kuan Yin and Buddha. They bring messages from our loved ones who have passed over too. Angels conduit to us divine love, divine intelligence, and divine healing. They can teach us about our own divinity, and help open us up to our magnificence, and our power.

Every day, write prayers or requests to your guardian angel. This morning, my son read me his angel prayers for the day. He is using these techniques too. I started crying happy tears as he shared his requests with me. Then I opened a new word document, and titled it My Angel Prayers, to save on my desktop. I have so many journals filled with my angel prayers, that I decided I wanted to keep them all in one place. I forget sometimes how much help I have received from the angels every day, especially when I'm in crisis, or moving, or starting a new career.

The angels have always helped me when I ask, and I know they are perfectly capable of helping you too. Having a journal, to read back your angel requests, is a wonderful tool, because when you are in times of uncertainty, you can re-read how much help you have received. In good times you can ask for even more and dream bigger. Reading your angel requests once a month is a great way to remember how much help you have received, and where you feel blocked.

As I edit this book in February, I sit in my new space in California, the angels brought me back from New Zealand after I did the first draft. Everything I wrote about in November I am living now.

Angels work quickly. For many years, I did not know my guardian angels name, I would say "angel's HELP please!" They always do. You do not need to know an angels name to receive help from him or her.

Many Kinds of Angels

There are many kinds of angels who specialize in various areas. In this chapter, you will meet four main angels. Then there are angels who sign up for different functions depending on their areas of expertise. There are the romance angels, the writing angels, the beauty angels, the weight loss angels, the fitness angels, painting angels, music angels, kitchen angels, and the housework angels just to mention a few. The housework angels won't magically appear and start cleaning your house – sorry! But they will clear your house of negative energy, and they will help you as you clean the house by making it seem less of a chore, while uplifting your spirit.

There are seventy-two angels who rule for twenty minutes each day, and for four days each year. These angels are ruled by the ten archangels in this book. These are the angels of astrology. Just as we have the western astrological system from the Greeks, so too do we have angel astrology where you are governed by different angel energy depending on the date of your birth.

You can ask for help from the angels with absolutely anything you are doing at any given time. Angels are your constant companions. They will help you in troubled times, and when things are great. Never worry that you are asking for help from too many angels. Once, when I was going through a difficult time, the angels told me they were sending 1500 angels to look after my family and myself. I thought that was a little excessive, but that was what they said. Another time they said seventy-two thousand angels. So, for the past year, I have been calling on seventy-two angels every day, as well as my guardian angel.

You too can call on angels all day long. Call on the fitness angels when you are exercising, the writing angels when you are writing, the communication angels when you need to talk about something, the protection angels when you leave the house, the romance angels for help with your love life.

There are so many different kinds of angels, and in this book, you will meet angels who specialize in seventy-two different areas. But, first let's start with the four most renown angels.

The four most well-known are Raphael, Michael, Gabriel and Uriel.

Raphael the Healer Angel

Raphael is the healer angel. He is the angel to call on when you need healing of any kind, physical, mental, emotional or spiritual. Raphael will heal the past, heal the present and even heal the future. He heals broken hearts, troubled relationships and disturbing situations. Whenever healing energy is required, ask him for help. He is the divine physician. Angel healing can happen in an instant. All you need to do for healing is to ask Raphael for help.

Close your eyes and picture him before you. I see Raphael wearing golden-yellow robes with long golden hair. If you have a situation from the past that needs healing, ask him to go back into the past with you, and heal the situation. You can ask him to heal a present situation, or a future one too. We will talk more about this in the chapter on the angels of healing.

He is the angel to call on for physical healing. Raphael means, God heals or divine health.

For now, think about what one thing would you like Raphael to help you with this week.

"I ask Raphael for healing with_____, dear Raphael I surrender this to your healing light."

Michael the angel of Courage and Le Coeur (The Heart)

Michael is the protector angel. He is like a huge security guard who stands outside of a nightclub. Michael is often shown carrying his sword. Sometimes he shows up in a velvet red cape, with flowing golden hair. His eyes are piercing. Michael is strong in his warrior training, and he leads his angelic army, the band of mercy with strength and grace. He is the angel of the heart chakra. His family is known as the Virtues.

Some traditions have Michael as the King of the Powers, much of our angel knowledge comes from the renaissance and middle ages. Spelling of angel's names can cause confusion for example, Michael and Mikael refer to the same angel. Haniel is spelt Haniel, Anael, Hanael or Aniel, she is the angel of joy or love. Her name means 'divine love'. El means of God or Divine. Haniel deriviations include: Anne, Grace, Grania, although Haniel is a male name in Jewish tradition because of Haniel's association with the planet Venus, she is known as the angel of love. The planet Venus rules Friday and is brings love, beauty and wisdom after the Roman Goddess she was named for. Anne is my middle name, Haniel is special to me and Grania, who I wrote about in Teen Goddess, is a Celtic sun Goddess and Grace O'Malley the infamous Irish Pirate ruled at the same time as Queen Elizabeth the first.

Michael embodies great leadership skills. He is the one to call on when you need help with deciding, or for any kind of protection whenever you feel unsafe.

If you are ever in a dangerous situation, or even one where you feel a little bit frightened, call out mentally "Michael, Help now!" He will be there instantly, and bring his band of mercy to help too.

Michael is the angel to call on if you are obsessing about negative things. If you are having trouble with addictions, nightmares or want to break your ties to the past, a person, place or thing. He will use his angelic sword to cut away all the etheric cords that keep you bound. You can ask Michael to give you a quick etheric dust-over each evening to clear away any psychic trash you have picked up during the day. You can ask Michael to open your heart to receiving more love and courage. Michael is the angel who hovers over the couple in the lover's card in the tarot. He knows all about matters of the heart, relationships, courage and protection.

Close your eyes and imagine Michael standing before you. What one thing would you like Michael to help you with this week? Ask him now.

Gabriel The Communication Angel

Gabriel is the messenger angel. She frequently shows up in the Bible and other holy texts bearing messages from God or the Divine for humans. She was the angel who told Mary she would give birth to Jesus. Gabriel loves music and beauty, and is often shown blowing her golden trumpet. Gabriel helps with spiritual sight too.

Gabriel was given a sex change in the middle ages at a papal council, when it was decreed that she was a male angel rather than a female one. She has always appeared female to me. Angels are genderless, but they each have certain character traits that can give them a more masculine or feminine feeling. Some people see Chamuel as male for example, but to me she shows up as a female. I never knew it was archangel Chamuel standing over my bed when I was three, until I saw a beautiful painting by Pamela Mathews on her website www.grail.co.nz. The painting was called "An Angel at My Window". She was identical to the angel I had been seeing for over forty years. Pamela very kindly sent me a beautiful silk screen print of Chamuel in 2013.

Gabriel is the angel to go to for help with communication of any kind. She will help if you are fighting with your loved ones. She can also help you with homework, write letters or emails, and with art and writing. She is the patron angel of musicians, writers, performing artists and spiritual counsellors.

Gabriel is the divine PR angel. She is a great angelic promoter, and will help you promote your cause, business, event, or yourself, if you ask her too. Call on Gabriel if you are feeling low in confidence. She is also the one to go to when you want to increase your ability to see angels. Every time I do a reading, a session with a client, or write my own angel prayers, I ask Gabriel for help.

What one thing would you like Gabriel to help you with this week? Ask Gabriel for help now.

Uriel The Angel of Catastrophes

Uriel's name means light of God. He is the angel who brings knowledge and understanding of the divine. Uriel is the angel of vision, he is sharp-sighted and can see far into the future. He can help you develop clear vision to see your life with clarity, and he will illuminate solutions for you when you are having difficulties. He will also give you pictures of what your life could be like if you took certain actions.

Uriel is the angel in the Bible whom God sent to Noah to warn him of the flood. He is the angel who came down from Heaven to the Garden of Eden on a sunbeam, and stood at the gate brandishing a fiery sword. Uriel is also the angel of natural catastrophes like hurricanes, storms, earthquakes and volcanoes. Whenever a crisis hits your life, call on Uriel for help. He knows what to do. He carries the flame of knowledge in his hand.

Uriel is an angel of justice and is a good angel to call on when you feel like someone has dumped on you. He can help explain things to you from a spiritual perspective, and will take care of divine retribution. Call on Uriel to help you see the divine plan of goodness for your life when everything seems a mess. Call on him to help you navigate through the difficulties in your life, and to help you take positive action to manifest your dreams.

What one thing would you like to ask Uriel to help you with this week? Ask Uriel for help now.

Angel Workout

Invoke the Four Angels

Do this exercise every morning and every evening for six weeks. It will help you develop a strong spiritual presence.

Close your eyes and see Raphael standing in front of you, Michael at your right, Gabriel behind you and Uriel at your left. See the archangels surrounding you with their strength, love and power. They create an angelic shield around you to protect you from harm.

The Angel Hierarchy

During the Middle Ages angels were divided by rank into nine orders like this:

1. Seraphim
2. Cherubim
3. Thrones
4. Dominions
5. Virtues
6. Powers
7. Principalities
8. Archangels
9. Angels

These are known as the choirs of angels, the orders or ranks of angels. Some traditions switch five and six. Michael and Raphael rule either five or six depending on which tradition you follow. Remember most modern angel knowledge comes from the middle ages or from western mysticism and has gone through several language changes as well as many cultural changes over the decades.

The numbers associated with each angel family is important because they correlate to the meaning in numerology as well as the numbers in the tarot. For example, Gabriel rules the Angels and Haniel rules the Principalities, Gabriel is associated with the number nine in numerology and the nine of cups, nine of swords, nine of wands, nine of pentacles in the tarot. Haniel carries the energy of seven and the seven of cups, seven of swords, seven of wands and seven of pentacles in the tarot. I included this knowledge for those of you who study tarot like I do.

Frequently asked questions

Are Angels real?

Absolutely!

How do you know they are real?

Good question. Okay, let me ask you a question. Do you believe in electricity? Can you see it? So how do you know it is real? Because you can see it working, right? With electricity, you can't see it, but you can see evidence of it. You know it works because when you plug a hairdryer into a socket and turn on the switch, the electricity comes through, and makes the hairdryer work.

The same principle works with the angels and the spiritual realms – you can tell they are there not so much by 'seeing' them, but by the evidence of their help in your life. And the way you see evidence is by asking for their help. Then look for the results in your life, and keep a journal of your experiences.

In 2010 the angels told me quite succinctly, "We are real, Catherine," they said. I heard it as loud as if you said it out loud right now. It was about 2.pm on a day in January when I was staying with my friends Jessica and Misha in New Zealand.

Why do angels want to help us?

They get great pleasure helping us. The angels say they love to help humans; it is part of their creative nature. Creating miracles is one of their favorite things to do. They love to create love, joy, laughter, happiness and lightheartedness. When humans are happy, they add to the total amount of happiness in the world, and everyone benefits. "When humans act from the spirits they act with love and compassion," say the angels. "Your planet can benefit from more of that now. The word for soul and breath come from the same source because they are one.

We will inspire you to act for good and with love. Love is an action, not a word. The Greeks had lots of words for it. Google it."

Apparently, the angels have heard of google, because they told me to google it as I was editing. I did, but that research is saved for my next angel book.

What about God? Do you have to believe in God to get help from the angels?

No, you don't need to believe in a deity or belong to a religious path. The angels can work in your life simply by you asking them to. They have no religious agenda – they work from a place of pure love. If you have a religious path that is special to you, then incorporate the angels into your life in a way that works best for you.

How can I see my angels?

Try this exercise to get you started:

Angel Workout

Close your eyes and imagine what your guardian angel looks like.

Just imagine. Sometimes people say, "I don't know what he or she looks like" when I ask them to do this. If that is how you are feeling now, then let me ask you this, close your eyes and imagine an orange, what does it look like? You can imagine, your imagination is your magic wand. Answer the following questions.

What would he or she look like if you did know? Just start describing him or her to me.

Write down what your angel looks like (make it up if you feel like you are getting nothing).

We will talk more about how to see angels further in the book.

How do angels talk to us?

There are many ways angels can communicate with you. You will learn different ways throughout this book. For now, just begin having mental conversations with your angels. Talk to them in your mind and imagine they are talking back to you.

What is the difference between an angel, a fairy and a spirit guide?

They are different species. Angels come in all shapes and sizes as do fairies, but they have a different energy feel to them; so, do spirit guides. I know this sounds vague, but when you work with angels, fairies and spirit guides, you can feel the difference in their energy, just like you feel the difference in different peoples' personalities.

Some fairies can be quite mischievous and aren't always concerned for your highest well-being. Not that they are mean-spirited or uncaring, but some of them are a little self-absorbed, and some like creating mischief. Like hiding things. Angels tend to be more responsible. Think of it this way - fairies will hide things, and the angels will help you find them.

There are seventy-two guardian angels. Each of these angel's rules for four days a year, twenty minutes a day, and is supervised by a "manager" angel. Think of this like a family of angels with one King or commanding angel in charge. The Dominions are one family for example, with Zadkiel as the royal leader of eight angels who have similar characteristics like earth families. My birth guardian angel is Iahhel, who rules January 26th to January 30th. Iahhel is under the rule of Raphael, who supervises The Archangels. You will learn more about this in the angel hierarchy.

How the angels can help you

I asked the angels if they could answer this, and here's what they said:

We are here to help you in so many ways dear one, here are just a few:

♥ To uplift and inspire you, to make your soul sing with delight...

♥ To provide comfort in times of sorrow, and to soothe your aching heart

♥ To illuminate your path, and hold a candle before you during dark days and times when you don't know which step to take, so you can see your path one step at a time

♥ To hold your hand on your soul's journey, and keep you company on this earthly path

♥ To help you manifest your dreams and heart's desires, to give you the tools and lead you to the resources you need to bring your dreams to fruition

♥ To connect you to the spiritual network bringing the right people, places and opportunities into your life that will lead to your highest good, and the highest good of all

♥ To recharge your spiritual batteries

♥ To remind you of your connection to god, the planet and your place in the universe

♥ To lighten your life with joy, laughter and fun

♥ As spiritual companions and friends so you need never be lonely

♥ As spiritual guidance counselors providing you with spiritual assistance and advice, as you live your life on this earthly plane

♥ To keep reminding you that you are a spiritual being having an earthly experience, and that there are spiritual solutions for all your problems

♥ To help you see things from a spiritual perspective rather than an earthly perspective

♥ To bring you tons of joy and happiness and help you to make your life more magical than you ever dreamed possible!

The angels say:

"There are so many things, dear one, that we can help you with. We want you to know that we love you very, very much, and that we are always with you. It gives us so much joy and happiness to help you. For when your heart is happy and sings, it makes our hearts sing too, and adds to the total amount of happiness and laughter in the world."

Keeping an angel journal

This is the single most important thing you can do to increase your awareness of the angels in your daily life. What you need is a blank book and a pen. You can buy a book with an angel on the front, or decorate it with stickers. This is your angel journal. Keep all your conversations with your angels in here. This is an invaluable tool. I have been keeping a journal since I was fourteen years old. Sometimes I will read answers that I got to questions I asked about a problem I was having, and it never ceases to amaze me how accurate the info from the angels is.

Six years before I became a mother I wrote about having a son named Logan and what he would look like. I forgot about it. When I was pregnant Logan's father and I bought a baby name book to look for names. We chose Logan. When Logan was two I found, the journal describing him.

Even today I forget amazing things that happen when I ask the angels for help. On Saturday night I wrote in my angel journal: *"Dear angels, please help us find the perfect place to live. Please let something wonderful open for us in the community I want to live in. Please let us know within seven days if we have a place or not."* The next morning there was an email from the community saying they had two places I could choose from in my inbox. When I went to write in my angel journal later that day, I saw the request I had made the night before. I had already forgotten I had written it. That is why it is so important to write things down, write down prayers, write down requests, pour your heart out to the angels. They love you and want to help you.

Having a track record by keeping a journal adds to your sense of faith and conviction. When people ask you if angels are real, you can start sharing your angel stories. The proof is in the evidence of what shows up in your life.

Angel Workout

- ♥ Get an angel journal to use with this book and begin writing to your angels every day for twenty minutes
- ♥ Write to your angels right now and introduce yourself, ask them a question and write down what you 'hear' as the answer, don't worry if it feels like you are making it up, write it anyway
- ♥ Write your favorite angel story in your angel journal
- ♥ Begin keeping notes of any angel experiences you have, sometimes writing bullet points is an easy way to track experiences too

DAY TWO. YOUR GUARDIAN ANGEL

Everyone has at least one guardian angel. Most angel experts say you have two. But whether you have ever felt your angel's presence or not, you have a guardian angel right by your side all the time. Your guardian angel has been with you from before you were born. He or she agreed to be your angel during your time on earth before you reincarnated on this planet. When you were still in the other world, you knew your guardian angel. He or she signed up to hover over you until you pass over to the other side again, when you will be reunited face-to-face.

Your guardian angel is with you from the time you are conceived until the time you exit the planet. Your guardian angel hovers around your mother while she is pregnant, and is there to welcome you into the world when you are born. He or she stays by your side throughout your life, and when you die, your angel is the first one to greet you as you pass over to the other side.

Everyone is born with access to at least three angels: your birth angel who rules over the day you were born; your heart angel who helps you on an emotional level, and your intellect angel who rules the time you were born. These angels are with you along with your guardian angel and angel guide.

Your guardian angel is here to guide and assist you. She acts as your number one cheerleader, your personal life coach and your spiritual trainer. Your guardian angel is your divine best friend. Always on the lookout for your highest good, he or she nudges you to reach for your dreams. Your guardian angel loves and supports you, and dispenses wise advice. You can share all your dreams, hopes, despair and deepest darkest secrets with your guardian angel. He will cheer you on when you act towards the dreams that are for your highest good and tap you on the shoulder when you veer off course.

Guardian angels can protect you from harm. They always seek your highest good, and encourage you to make the choices that will lead to that. Your guardian angel is by your side always. She gently flitters around you, at times frantically waving her hands to get your attention.

My dictionary defines a guardian angel as: A guardian angel is a spirit who protects and guides a particular person. The concept of patron angels and their hierarchy was extensively developed in Christianity in the 5th century by Pseudo-Dionysius the Areopagite. The theology of angels, and tutelary spirits, has undergone many refinements since then, and contemporary orthodox belief in both the eastern and western churches is that guardian angels protect the body and present prayers to God, protecting whichever person God assigns them to. The Roman Catholic Church calendar of saints includes a memorial for guardian angels on October 2nd.

The belief that God sends a spirit to watch every individual was common in Ancient Greek philosophy, and Plato alludes to it in Phaedo. Similarly, the belief appears in the Old Testament. The first Christian theologian to outline a specific scheme for guardian angels was Honorius of Autun. He said that every soul was assigned a guardian angel the moment it was put into a body, although such a thought requires the pre-existence of the soul/essence. Scholastic theologians augmented and ordered the arrangement of angel guardians. Thomas Aquinas agreed with Honorius and specified that it was the lowest order of angels who served as guardians, and his view was most successful in popular thought, but Robert Duns Scotus said that any angel might accept the mission.

Much of today's knowledge of angels comes from the Middle Ages. Angels were popular in the Middle Ages, and appeared all over the place; in the media, in art and in discussions just as they do today. Theologians and philosophers would discuss such questions as what are angels made of, do they live forever, do they have free will and do they evolve to higher spiritual realms. Can you imagine a group of white collar business people sitting around talking about such things today?

Life in the Middle Ages was different from life as we know it now. For one thing, the Catholic Church was the governing force and made decisions about nearly every facet of daily life that affected common people. Secondly, media in the middle ages was much different than media today. There was no internet or printing press, therefore, no newspapers, magazines or books of mass production. The few books that did exist were handwritten by monks, and kept in monasteries. Most people couldn't read simply because there were no books for them to read. The forms of media that did exist in the Middle Ages were sermons, prayers, stained glass windows, art, lectures and icons.

Stained glass windows adorned the interior of churches not only to look beautiful, but also to tell a story much like a picture book or comic strip with each picture window building on the window before. Icons were painted on wood, and were used as meditation tools to make direct contact with the being represented. If you had an icon with a picture of an angel, you could gaze at the picture and connect to the energy of the angel. Today, people use tarot cards or angel cards in much the same way.

Lectures were a major source of entertainment for people in the Middle Ages. People would go see lectures in big venues, and hotly discuss the topic and points made with their friends on the way home afterwards, just like when you see a movie or Ted talks today. One of the most famous lecturers was Thomas Aquinas, who was also known as the angelic doctor, because his knowledge of Angels was so great.

Thomas lectured about fifteen times each week. He was made a saint less than fifty years after he died.

Thomas was an Italian theologian who specialized in the study of angels, although he never had a single direct experience with angels himself. All his knowledge came from reading the Bible, and from the depth of his own education and intellect.

He believed that angels were pure intellect, that they didn't have a body, but that they could appear in human form at will. He thought each angel was a separate species and a unique being, rather than belonging to an 'angelic race.' Thomas believed that angels came from a higher sphere than humans. His train of thought was the most popular in its time.

Another angel expert was John Dun Scotus. John believed angels were a distinct species, or race of beings, made up of spiritual matter. He thought angels could think and reason just like humans do, only they were more perfect (or divine) in their thinking and reasoning. John said each angel had his or her own personality, and that angels were higher on the spiritual hierarchy than humans, but approachable to humans as intercessors between the earthly realm and the spiritual realms. He believed angels were like humans in appearance, but made of finer matter. After the Middle Ages there was not much discussion about angels anymore, mainly because both men had debated about angels so thoroughly there was not much else left to discuss.

In the 1990s angels enjoyed another renaissance. There were programs like Touched by An Angel, which came out in 1994 and ran for eleven seasons, and movies like Michael, portraying archangel Michael doing various tasks on earth played by a cigarette smoking John Travolta in 1996. The 90s brought in a new era of angel knowledge. More people were writing about the direct experiences they had with angels.

Angel expert Doreen Virtue has written many angel books since her first book on angels came out in 1997, and has trained many people around the world to become Angel Therapy Practitioners. Doreen has written over fifty books and oracle decks about angels, she could be considered the angel doctor of this era.

This is the traditional Christian prayer to one's guardian angel.

Angel of God, my guardian dear

to whom God's love commits me here.

Ever this day/night be at my side

to light and guard, to rule and guide.

Amen.

While John Dun Scotus and Thomas of Aquinas wrote, and lectured extensively about angels during the Middle Ages, angels, like humans and planets are always evolving. I believe everything in our multiverse is always evolving, and it is silly to think things are static. The planet Chiron was discovered in 1997. Our universe is ever expanding, always evolving and now that people can read and have access to so much information thanks to the internet and books, more and more people are having direct experience with angels.

Everybody has a guardian angel. It is my experience that everyone has one primary guardian angel. Other angels may come and go during your life, but your primary guardian angel always stays with you.

Sometimes deceased loved ones like your grandparents or pet may sign up to watch over you too. You may be surrounded by a whole host of angels who are helping you. You may have the study angels, the protection angels and the romance angels working with you as well as your grandmother, your pet and an Archangel, plus your guardian angel.

Most people have at least six angels assisting them on any given day, if you have asked for their help. During the day, you may receive help from different angels. For example, you may call on the homework angels to help you while you are doing your homework, the diet and exercise angels to help you while you are working out and the protection angels to watch over you while you are sleeping. Once you have finished the specific task that the angels specialize in, they will be off and come back to visit you when next you request their help.

Think of your home as an angel hangout with angels constantly coming and going. The area around your body is like this too. Some angels will stick around for a few months, even years. Like the romance angels, if you ask for their help to attract a soulmate, and create a soul relationship, they may stay with you for many years teaching you about the various aspects of love. Like how to love, how to receive love and counseling you about your relationships.

Your guardian angel is always with you. He or she is the one constant angel throughout your life. Just knowing your guardian angel is always with you can be a great comfort. You need never be lonely again.

How to talk with your guardian angel

Your guardian angel will talk with you in a multitude of different ways. The most common is through telepathy. Telepathy is the art of having mental conversations. You receive impressions, pictures, words, thought waves or feelings through your mind. To talk to your guardian angel, simply start a conversation with him or her in your mind. You will learn about telepathic communication on day fifteen. For now, practice asking your guardian angel questions in your mind. If you can talk to yourself mentally, you can talk to your angels mentally too.

Angel workout

Ask your guardian angel three questions. They can be questions about anything. Then write down what you "imagine" your guardian angel is saying. Some examples of questions are:

- ♥ What is my divine life purpose?
- ♥ Angels, how will you communicate with me?
- ♥ Angels, how can I see you better?
- ♥ What is your name?
- ♥ What do I need to do to get through this...?
- ♥ What steps can I take about ...?
- ♥ How can I heal my relationship with...?

Write the answers below or in your angel journal. Listen to your guardian angel, and write down what you think you hear. Don't worry if it feels like you are making it up. Do it anyway.

Most people feel like they are making it up at first. How do you distinguish between actual angel guidance and your imagination? The angels will talk to you through your imagination, this is one of the ways they can communicate with you. So, it is very important that you don't discount things as being "all in your imagination". Your imagination is one of your most important spiritual tools.

Write your questions and answers below:

Do this meditation when you can set aside thirty minutes of uninterrupted time.

Meditation to meet your guardian angel

To begin you might like to put some meditation music on sit while you read this with the headphones on. Read one paragraph at a time, and then close your eyes and imagine what you have read taking place before you move on to the next paragraph.

Begin to breathe deeply. You are about to begin an exciting journey. One that will take you to the heavenly realms to meet with your guardian angel. Take several deep breaths in and out. As you breathe in imagine white light with sparkling golden flecks entering the top of your head and traveling down your spinal cord. This light becomes stronger and stronger, and more brilliant, until you feel your whole body immersed in this beautiful divine light. You feel your body now as an ocean of energy.

You begin to feel very, very relaxed and very, very light. More light enters your body now than it has ever contained before. You feel every cell in your body being transformed with this beautiful divine liquid light.

Before you, you see a beautiful sparkling bridge of light. You begin to walk towards this bridge. As you cross the bridge, you feel all your worries and concerns from the day fall away from you gently and effortlessly. You know once you have crossed the bridge, you will reach the heavenly kingdom where the angels reside. You begin to feel a sense of excitement knowing today is the day you will make conscious contact with your guardian angel.

Now you find yourself in a beautiful meadow filled with lush waterfalls, fields of spring flowers and brilliant blue skies. You stand on the ground and mentally call your guardian angel to appear before you.

"Guardian angel, please be here now!"

Your guardian angel appears instantly before you. You look into your guardian angel's eyes and feel an instant connection. Whatever image appears before you, you know that is the perfect representation of your guardian angel. You look deeply into the eyes of your guardian angel. Your heart is open with gratitude and love, and you feel that you are in the presence of a divine being. You feel the warmth of divine love and divine light surround you.

Your guardian angel asks you if you would like to receive a transmission of healing energy from him or her. If so, you reply "yes." Your guardian angel asks you to hold your hands out, palms facing upwards, and to breathe deeply. You place your hands as asked, and begin taking deep breaths. Your guardian angel sends a laser beam of light from his or her eyes into your eyes, a laser beam of light and love from his heart to your heart and a laser beam of light from his or her hands into the palms of your hands. You feel your body tingle as it receives this outpouring of divine light and love.

Your angel gently places her hands upon your shoulders and says: "*My child, I have been with you since before you were born, and I will be with you until the day you die. I am always by your side, available to help and to guide you, to encourage and comfort you. All you have to do whenever you have a need is simply call on me.*"

You feel your heart melt into the love your angel is offering you. You ask your guardian angel a question. Spend some time hanging out with your guardian angel continuing a conversation, and when you are ready, come back to this time and this place and the room you are in.

People sometimes ask me if guardian angels have special angelic sounding names. Some do, some don't. Once I was doing an angel reading for a man who wanted to know the name of his guardian angel. I was encouraging him to ask his guardian angel what his name was. My client kept saying: "Nothing is coming. I'm not getting a name." I had a feeling that he was, but didn't want to tell me because he was afraid it wasn't 'right', or that he was just 'making it up.'

I blurted out: "The name that I am getting is Frank!"

He looked up and said: "That's the name I've been getting too!"

It doesn't matter what your guardian angel is called. What is more important is the essence you feel when you call on him or her.

What does your guardian angel look like?

Most people can see their guardian angel a lot more clearly than they think they can. Some months ago I was doing a psychic reading for a client who wanted to see her guardian angel. I led her through a guided meditation, much like the one I wrote for you. Then I asked her what her angel looked like. She said she wasn't sure, and that she was having trouble picturing him. I began to ask her questions as if she did know. Soon she could give me a fairly complete description of her angel. Let's try this exercise now.

Angel Workout

This is a great exercise to begin to get a sense of what your guardian angel looks like.

I want you to describe to me what your guardian angel looks like. Do this exercise quickly and write down the first thing that comes to mind.

Ask your guardian angel to come to you, say: *"Dear guardian angel of mine, please be here now."* It doesn't matter if you can't picture him or her, just get a sense of, or a feeling that your angel is close by. If you don't feel like you 'see' anything, don't worry, make it up as you go along. Your imagination is an accurate receptor for telepathic information.

What color hair does your guardian angel have?

How tall is he or she?

What color eyes does he or she have?

What does his body look like, or what shape is she?

Now begin to let a sharper image form in your imagination. Zoom in with your mind and begin to see your angel in more detail.

Tell me what kind of facial structure does your angel have?

Is his or her face round or angular? Heart-shaped or oval? What kind of cheekbones does she have? Is his chin pointy or rounded?

Describe your angel in as much detail as possible. Write your description down in your angel journal.

Now ask your guardian angel his or her name. Write down whatever comes to mind.

Angel Workout:

Make an appointment to see your guardian angel.

Set aside some time to spend with your guardian angel, the only way you are going to get to know him or her is by spending time with them – just like with people. Twenty minutes each day is a good schedule. Tell your angel ahead of time that you have made this commitment, and then be sure to keep it. For example, you could decide that every day this week at 7pm, you will talk to your guardian angel for twenty minutes. Put your appointment down in your phone or calendar to make it 'official'. Then make it a priority, just like you would make it a priority if you had an important business meeting.

You see, if you want to have a good quality on-going relationship with your guardian angel, you need to put energy into it. This means getting quiet and talking to him or her, then listening to what she wants to say. The evidence that it is angelic dictation is when you look back later, and see the results that have shown up. For now, just trust the process and have faith that your angel is with you, helping you and guiding you.

Make a commitment to your relationship with your guardian angel. Remember the only way you are going to get to know him or her better is by spending time with her. Practice having mental conversations with your guardian angel throughout the day. Call on your guardian angel for help regularly. Simply say "guardian angel help me with this now".

Practice asking your guardian angel questions and listening for the answer. Write down what you think you hear, even if it feels like you are making it up. Begin to keep a record of what your guardian angel says, and read it at the end of the week.

DAY THREE. YOUR ANGEL GUIDE

What is the difference between your guardian angel and your angel guide? Good question. I asked the angels myself, and this is what they said:

"Your guardian angel is your best friend in the angelic world. Your guardian angel is always with you. As you know there is a guardian angel assigned to every blade of grass, every star in the sky, and of course every human on this planet. Most of you have two guardian angels.

Your angel guide is also with you from the time you are born until the time you exit the planet.

You have many guides, soul guides, spirit guides, animal guides, deceased loved ones who are with you in spirit form to continue a relationship with you until you pass over and greet them again."

The angels say: *"Unfortunately, many people in your realm are disconnected from their spiritual source. They think of themselves as human beings rather than spiritual beings having a human experience.*

"This is very sad to us as you have so much spiritual help and power at your disposal. If you would just start asking for help, and learning to tune in every day to your guardian angel and your angel guide, you would never feel lonely or uncertain again."

Your angel guide gives you clear guidance on every aspect of your life. Your angel guide is your personal travelling companion from the angelic realm to help you navigate through this earthly realm. Your angel guide is assigned to guide you whereas your guardian angel is assigned to guard, protect, nurture and comfort you. Both play important roles in your life, and both work together for your highest good.

You always have free choice. That is part of the human experience. So, you can choose to listen to your angels' advice and insight, or do something completely different. Remember that you are constantly in the process of creating your future. I like to picture it as if you are standing in a lobby with five different doorways in front of you; you can choose any doorway to venture through. Each doorway is an opening to a probable future.

When you ask your angels for guidance and advice they help you gain insight and clarity to what is for your highest good. It may not always be easy to act and follow their guidance, but they will never set you astray. Sometimes you may have to follow their guidance day-by-day, sometimes you may have to follow minute-by-minute, especially if you are in a low point in your life. Don't be afraid. The angels promise to love you and guide you no matter what stage your life is at. You always have help available.

Guardian Angels

My dictionary defines a guardian as a person who cares for a person, people or property.

My dictionary defines a guardian angel as an angel to protect and assist a particular person. The belief in angels can be traced through all antiquity and exist in every culture and every religion.

Angel Guide

My dictionary defines guide as:

Someone employed to conduct others.

Someone who can direct the course, or determine the direction of travelling.

Someone who shows the way by leading, or advising.

Be a guiding or motivating force.

Someone who can find paths through unexplored territory.

Now do you understand the difference between your guardian angel and your angel guide? They both love you and have specific functions. They will willingly work with you when you ask them to. The more often you ask, the happier they are. They also appreciate gratitude for the work they do. A simple *"thank you, dear angels"* brings them great joy.

Are you open for guidance?

As a psychic reader and an angel channel, I have taught people how to connect with their own angels, or act as a conduit for someone who is having a hard time tuning into their angels. Lots of people will tell you they are ready for guidance, and they want guidance, but then never follow the guidance they are given.

This frustrates your angel guide. I promise you, your life will run smoother and more joyfully if you tune in everyday for five minutes to ask your angel guide what to do that day. Each morning when you wake up ask your angel guide: *"What would you like me to do today, dear angel guide?"* You can also say the following prayer: *"Dear angel guide, please lead me to the people, places and opportunities that are for my highest good. Help me to navigate through the day with divine assistance."*

Talk continually to your angel guide throughout the day. Sometimes you may feel prompted to drive home a different way from work, go to a certain store, or to buy a certain type of food. That is one of the ways your angel guide will help you navigate through your day.

When you are in a crisis your angel guide will gently help, taking you by the hand minute-by-minute, and patiently loving you and walking you through your experience.

We all go through unexplored territory at some stage of our lives: the first time we fall in love, the first time we leave home, the first time someone close to us dies, the first time someone betrays us. Each time your angel guide is there to hold your hand and be a guiding force, illuminating the path before you so you can take the very next step that will be for your highest good.

Your angel guide can be there when you are at a particularly low point in your life, like a client of mine whose husband was arrested for battery against her. It turned into a five-year legal nightmare, because her husband was so abusive. There were many times she felt like giving up. Some days, things seemed to just get worse and worse, and it seemed there was no light at the end of this tunnel. There were many times she questioned her faith, or wondered why she had been spared a life-threatening illness three months before her husband was arrested. *"If I had known what was to come, I probably would have chosen to leave the planet then! I could hear my angels telling me it wasn't my time, yet when I was sick, I laughed with them then, saying I know. What came afterwards was the worst time of my life, and I felt like the angels played a cruel joke on me."*

It's okay to be angry at your angels or feel that way, because sometimes we have limited perspective during a crisis. That's when we need to cling to our faith the most. The experience my client had led her back to her life's work, which was teaching and writing, something she thought she would never have been able to do within the context of her marriage.

When you are going through a crisis, remember, this isn't the end of the story. One tool I use is to remind myself the story of my life hasn't been finished yet. As you turn the page of each day, you will find ups and downs, and when everything appears dismal, know that there is a reason you are going through this (as clichéd as that sounds). It may not be apparent yet, but it will be. Your angel guide is right there with you to help you navigate the steps of your life. Remember to ask, ask, ask. The more you get into the practice of asking the more you will connect with the angelic realm and the more divine assistance you will receive.

Your angel workout

We have covered a lot of material today. Your homework for today is to tune into your angel guide using the techniques you have learned so far. Tomorrow we will be covering different ways angels communicate with us in more depth. So for now set aside fifteen minutes to talk to your angel guide.

Ask her her (or his) name.

Ask her what she looks like.

Spend some time asking her questions about herself as if you were getting to know a new friend, just like you did with your guardian angel.

And throughout your day, keep asking your angel guide to guide you to the people, places and opportunities, that will best assist you. This is the start of your relationship with your angel guide.

Pay attention today to any synchronicities, coincidences or joyful happenings, notice what lifts your spirits and what dampens it.

Write about your experience below.

DAY FOUR. ANGEL SIGNS FOR YOU

Angels love to help you.

You have access to so much help from the angelic kingdom. You have your guardian angel, your angel guide, your birth angel, your heart angel and your intellect angel. Your birth angel rules the day you were born, your heart angel rules your emotions and your intellect angel rules the time that you were born. You can simply say "angels help" whenever you need their help.

My favorite prayer is: "Angels lead me to the people, places and opportunities that will best help me." You can make it more specific like: "Angels lead me to the perfect doctor that will best help me with _____" or, "Angels please lead me to the perfect job opportunity that will best utilize my skills and services" or, "Angels, may the people who will best benefit from my services find me."

How do you talk to angels?

The primary way you talk to angels is through your mind. Simply start a mental conversation with them. Conversation implies they will talk back to you, otherwise you would just be talking *at* them. Tell the angels, especially your guardian angel, whatever is on your heart and in your mind. Talk to them like you talk to your best friend. The angels love indulging in angelic gossip. They will happily give you the latest in heavenly news. They will eagerly share suggestions on how to improve your life and pass on divine messages.

Speak out loud to your angels when you are alone. If you talk out loud to them around other people, they might think you are nuts! With angels, you need never be lonely. They make great companions when driving alone, doing your grocery shopping or just hanging out at home. Angels have different personalities just as humans do, some are chatterboxes, some are more serious, the main difference is they always operate from a place of pure love and pure light. If you have held an image of angels as serious somber beings who only talk when they have something important to say, throw that image out the window now.

Write out all your concerns and desires to the angels. Keep an angel journal where you can record all your requests and desires and then jot down the replies you get. When you reread your journal six months later, you will be amazed at how much the angels help you once you start asking. The main reason I wrote this book in workbook form is to kick-start you with your angel journal daily writing practice. In my private practice, I always advocate keeping an angel journal so you will see evidence of how much help shows up for you when you ask. What I have found is sometimes people don't know how or where to start – thus the workbook you are holding in your hands. When you finish working through this book, it is my hope you will continue to keep an angel journal for the rest of your life.

What is a mental conversation? It is a conversation you have inside your head. Have you ever had the experience of rehearsing a conversation you are about to have with a boss or a loved one? Or of replaying a conversation you had with someone over and over in your mind? Those are examples of mental conversations. The very first question clients often ask me is: 'How do I know I'm not just making it up when I write down what I think my angels are telling me?" That is why it is so important for you to keep a journal. You will record things there that will show up as evidence for you that the angels are listening to your requests and you are receiving answers.

I am thinking now of a mental conversation I was having with the angels as I went through the second year of my divorce. I was walking by the grocery shop and lamenting the fact about how I didn't really want to be divorced, and couldn't we just give it one more try? I walked straight into a four by two sticking out of someone's truck. The angels can be quite literal in their communication with you. Being whacked over the head with a four by two block of wood, and landing on my back in the grocery store car park, was not much fun. I got a concussion, but I got a definite NO to any answer. Lucky for me the angels were protecting me from things I did not yet know. Some people might say: "Well, why didn't they protect you in the first place by letting you know not to marry?"

Two reasons: One: We are given divine guidance and divine messages for a reason, but we don't always follow it. Falling in love is one of the trickiest times for tuning in to your psychic guidance. Two: The feeling of falling in love is so intoxicating, that it can override rational reason. I got very strong guidance my marriage was not a good idea. But we live in a world of polarity where we grow through so-called mistakes, just as we grow can grow through joy.

You can lie to a psychic. Many people are under the impression that if you are psychic or empathetic you read minds. Readers are always reading, sometimes when falling in love psychics doubt themselves especially if they have a history of trauma.

Your guardian angel has many ways of showing you signs that he or she has received your messages. Some common signs are physical symbols showing up like hummingbirds, white feathers, coins, and so on, depending on which culture you are in. One of my clients knew her ex-boyfriend, who had died of cancer, was communicating with her when she kept seeing two white doves everywhere. Those were their favorite birds, and had symbolic meaning for them. Over the next four days, you will learn specific ways the angels will communicate to you. These are primarily through your physical senses, and your spiritual senses. Sometimes people think you must be a space cadet to get angel messages. The opposite is true. You need to be more in your body, more grounded. You must be able to walk in two worlds, this earthly realm, and the intuitive non-analytical realm; the realm of the imagination, trust and faith.

Trust and faith are easy when you are looking for a parking space or a green light, and ask the angels for one, and one shows up. When you have major life decisions to make, your life is on the line, or whether you are worrying about where your next meal is coming from, trust and faith can be harder to practice. When you are desperate, an angel sign can give you hope to cling on to.

I have seen clients getting emails from long-lost loved ones that came at just the right time. Angels signs can range from tangible symbols to emails, texts, or phone calls of support. Here are some of the ways the angels will show their support for you:

- Coins
- White feathers
- Emails, texts, unexpected messages from friends (and even strangers sometimes)
- Money in just the amount you need it. I have seen people get checks anywhere from a hundred dollars to twenty thousand dollars show up from unexpected sources
- Hummingbirds, butterflies, seagulls, crickets, dragonflies,
- Rainbows

When you see signs of symbolic reminders that the angels are with you, these are simply signs that the angels have received, and are in the process, of co-creating opportunities for you.

For communicating with the angels, you will receive messages through your ears, your eyes, your imagination, your intuition, precognition, body chills and sensations and all sorts of different ways. Each day, we will build on a new skill set.

Angel workout:

What is a way you have received signs from angels before?

What is a way someone you know has received a sign from an angel?

When I left Albuquerque to go to Huntington Beach, it was a huge move for me. I was selling the family home I had raised my sons in. I had a business. I had clients. I was teaching a law of attraction class that had over 600 members. It was a big decision to make. I had lived in that house for over twenty years. Many of my sons' friends grew up there too. I wanted to leave Albuquerque, leave everything behind, and have a fresh start. But it was also terrifying not knowing if I was doing the right thing. Not quite the same as looking for a car park or a green light!

I prayed about it so much asking for guidance. I received many angel signs that I was on the right path, including getting a new license plate the week we were leaving, with the three digits of the new zip code I was moving to on it. While walking into my office to store some things on the day I was leaving, a new client showed up out of the blue for a reading. I apologized profusely that I couldn't do a session as I was leaving to drive to Huntington Beach. Turned out that was where she was from. She had come to Albuquerque for a vacation. When I arrived in Huntington Beach she gave me an angel picture to remind me the angels had brought her to me.

When I was deciding to leave New Zealand, I asked for signs again. My health was not 100 percent. I had surgery in July for an ankle I broke in three places where my foot was cut open and plates inserted. The day after I made the decision my editor called me to ask me if I wanted to talk in Las Vegas. I received many signs I was doing the right thing.

The angels can, and will, give you confirmation that you are on the right track.

They will also give you whacks over the head (quite literally) when you are going off track.

Angel Workout

How to ask the angels for a sign:

1. Close your eyes and relax
2. Start Breathing deeply
3. Imagine your guardian angel standing directly in front of you
4. Ask: *"Dear guardian angel, please show me a sign that you are real within seven days. Show me the sign I will see to know that you exist."*
5. Whatever random image or object comes to mind, don't judge it, just observe it. I have had clients see a bag of groceries, purple feathers, money, smiling white cats, red roses, yellow flowers, a sequence of numbers.
6. Write down whatever image first came to mind below.
7. Wait for it to show up within seven days.

Sometimes even I get cynical. I re-tested this workout this week, before adding it to this workbook. Last Sunday I did the above steps, and three images popped into my head - a purple feather, red roses, and black and white fluffy cats or dogs. The next morning I got on Facebook, and my friend James had posted a photo of a bunch of red roses on my page and written: "For you Catherine". James has never done that before, and I have known him for twenty years.

So, I was like; "Okay Angels, thank you for that." I walked outside to go to the market, and right in the middle of the sidewalk was a big, fat, gorgeous, fluffy, white cat with blue eyes, literally lying on the path so I couldn't get past her, and smiling up at me.

"Thank you, angels, for sign two," I say.

I was thinking a purple feather seemed a bit far-fetched, and in my head, it had looked like a deliberately dyed purple feather, rather than one from a bird. I was cynical about seeing that. I thought: "Well, maybe it might show up over the course of the week – who knows?"

Lo and behold, on my way back from the market, I am walking down my street, and I see this car parked near my house with three feathers dangling from the car inside mirror. Two are black and green bird feathers from the Tui, which is a native New Zealand bird. Tui in mythology means singing your life song, overcoming fear and expressing your inner gifts. Her energy is like Mockingbirds. Birds are considered spiritual messengers in many traditions because of their ability to fly.

What color was the third? It was dyed purple and pink. Pink is the color of my aura. I nearly fell over. This was the day after I had asked what signs my guardian angel would give me to show me she was with me, and cared about me. "THANK YOU, Angels"

Angel workout for today:

Do the above angel workout, what angel sign did you get in your mind?

Don't judge how unrealistic, silly, simplistic or random it is. Most people usually get one sign to look out for, not three!

Over the next seven days wait for it to show up, and when it does, write about it below, and remember to thank your guardian angel.

The morning of the seventh day since I got the purple feather message, I walked out of my house and again, nearly fell over.

This was on my neighbor's fence. If I had walked out a minute later, they would have been taken down. The angels love to show what they are capable of, so start asking.

Angel Workout

Find some relaxing alpha music on YouTube. I like yellow brick cinema's channel for these exercises.

Sit down, relax, close your eyes and listen to a piece of music with alpha waves. Count backwards from ten to one. Take long slow deep breaths and feel your entire body relax.

Ask your guardian angel, "my dear guardian angel, please show me a sign you will give me within seven days that I can look for to know you are real and with me." See what picture pops into your mind. Don't judge it. Over the next seven days be on the lookout for your sign to show up.

Use this technique when you need reassurance the angels are with you, if you have an important decision to make and want to know if you are on the right track or whenever your intuition tells you to do this.

DAY FIVE. HOW TO RECEIVE PICTURES FROM THE ANGELS

Mental pictures come in the form of images, movies, scenes and visions. Mental pictures are one form of communication the angels can use to talk to you. The angels can send you mental pictures to warn you of danger, inform you of upcoming events, transmit information, encouragement or the answer to a problem.

The primary way we communicate with ourselves is through mental pictures. Throughout the day we are constantly running movies in our inner mind. These movies consist of stories we tell ourselves about the past, the present and the future. People who worry a lot tend to play movies in their minds that focus on their failures or mistakes. When they think of the future, they tend to play horror movies, imagining the worst possible outcomes of whatever they are involved in.

People with an optimistic outlook tend to play movies that are hopeful, positive, and that have a successful outcome. They see themselves succeeding, and learning at whatever they undertake.

You can choose what kind of movies you view in your mind, just as easily as changing the channel on TV. When you play inner movies that are happy, joyous and where you see yourself succeeding, these are the kind of life experiences you will draw to you through the law of attraction. Because you are made from energy, your vibration will attract energy of a similar vibration. So, if you don't like your current life circumstances, all you have to do is change your vibe, and immediately you will start to attract different circumstances.

Angel Workout

See yourself as the star of your own life movie. You are the star, the writer, the director and the casting agent. Imagine everyone in your life is there because you cast them in your life story. The roles of villains, love interests, friends, foes and heroes have all been assigned by you. All the situations – challenges and opportunities, good times and bad - have also been written into your life. You are the main actor in this story, and you are the narrator.

Anytime you like, you can choose to change your point of view, and rewrite the situation from a different perspective. You can rewrite each situation as a comedy, a tragedy, a drama, a mystery or a romance. You can fire any of the other 'actors' at any time you wish. You can write characters out, and write new characters in. You can direct the story of your life to be the greatest story of all time, and you can act with whatever qualities you desire.

In your imagination, play a mental movie of your life exactly the way you would love it to be. Create mental pictures and mental movies that are fun and bring you joy. Transport yourself in your imagination to places you have always wanted to visit.

Anytime a negative picture comes to mind, change it into one that is fun and joyous. See yourself happy and enjoying life, surrounded by people you love, doing activities you love. Write a list of five or six happy pictures that you can bring to mind whenever you find yourself creating unhappy mental pictures. Post this list on your bathroom mirror.

Now you are going to do an exercise to begin receiving mental pictures from the angels. It is best not to try this after eating a large meal as food is very grounding.

Here are the steps you will follow

1. Get relaxed
2. Clear your mind
3. Clear your emotions

4. See your mental screen
5. Open to receive images or pictures
6. Ask the angels to start transmitting pictures to you
7. Begin to receive

Step one: Get Relaxed, put relaxing music on, lie down or sit in a comfortable chair and begin to breathe deeply. Breathing slowly will naturally calm your emotions. Count down from ten to one instructing your mind to go deeper into relaxation with every breath you take.

Step two: Clear your mind, Picture your mental screen as blank. Any thoughts easily dissolve and do not distract you from your purpose. You feel calm and relaxed. Allow your mind to enter a deeply meditative state.

Step three: Clear your emotions. Imagine your emotions as lines of light that travel along a similar circuit as your circulatory system. See these lines of light as smooth and flowing harmoniously, instruct your emotions to calm and relax. Breathe out any distressing thoughts, and breathe in divine light. Continue to do this for as long as it takes for you to feel calm.

Step four: See your mental screen. Picture a screen in your imagination. This is your mental screen. Right now, imagine this screen is blank. This screen will be the receiving center for visual impressions from your angels.

Step five: Open to receive images or pictures. Tune into your inner vision. With your inner eyes, you have expanded awareness. You can see behind you, beneath you, above you and further out in front of you than ever before.

Feel your mind relax and instruct it to open. If you like, you can imagine a window in the middle of your forehead that gently opens to allow angelic imprints to enter. Do not fear that you may receive frightening images. If this ever happens, you can ask Michael, the archangel of protection, to remove them immediately.

Step six: Ask the angels to start transmitting pictures to you. Simply ask: 'Dearest angels, I am now ready to receive visual impressions from you, please begin to transmit whatever images will best help me at this time."

You can ask for pictures relating to a problem or a question you may have.

State your question here and open to receive.

Imagine your guardian angel standing in front of you. She begins sending you pictures into your mind telepathically. You receive these pictures on your mental screen.

Step seven: Begin to receive. You are now receiving images upon your mental screen. Take note of what these are, spend ten minutes receiving images, and then when you are ready, instruct your mind to come back to your normal waking state saying out loud, "I will feel healthy and alert and better than before I began this meditation."

Angel Workout

Write about your experience in your angel journal. What kinds of visual impressions did you receive? Did you see colors or patterns of energy? Did you see scenarios playing out on your mental screen or did you see still pictures? Did words or symbols show up instead?

There is no right or wrong way to receive pictures from your angels. Sometimes you may sense something rather than see it. Do not be discouraged if you felt like you weren't seeing anything. Keep practicing and trust that the more you practice, the more skilled you will become.

DAY SIX. HOW TO SEE ANGELS

Have you ever wondered what an angel looked like? Or have you seen an angel? Many people who love angels want to be able to see them too. Some people are afraid to see angels in case they see something bad. But in my experience angels always show up with a warm feeling of love and bliss.

Your Spiritual Senses

We each have five spiritual senses as well as our five physical senses. These are commonly called clairvoyance, clairaudience, clairsentience and claircognition. I call them spiritual sight, spiritual hearing, spiritual feeling and spiritual knowing. Just like you may have one or two physical senses that are more dominant than your other senses, so it is with your spiritual senses. It is common to have one spiritual sense that is more dominant in you than others.

The prefix clair means clear in French, clear seeing is another word for clairvoyance, clear hearing for clairaudience, clear feeling for clear sentience and clear knowledge for claircognition. Your spiritual senses bring you clarity, insight and guidance.

The fifth psychic sense is intuition or ESP extraordinary sensory perception, which simply means your senses are heightened and you have a high level of psychic ability or intuitive knowing.

Today you will learn how to use your spiritual sight to see angels. Artists in the renaissance and middle ages are responsible for many of the images we hold in our head of angels with halos and wings. And many of the images come from people's creative interpretation, from biblical passages, and from seeing angels yourself. Often it is easier to feel the presence of angels than it is to see them. This is because angels vibrate at a higher frequency than humans. Their energy is lighter and less dense than our human bodies.

What do angels look like?

Guardian angels often show up traditionally being about seven feet tall, hovering about two feet off the ground with large wings, attired in long white robes with a golden halo. The halo looks very much like the glow around a light bulb or candle. Some people think that the halo is the angel's aura. Yes, angels have auras too, and specific colors, just as humans do. That is why they can show up as colors when you are learning to see them. Plus their energy moves quickly and can look like flashes of light.

Angels are energy, pure energy, just like all matter in the universe. Their energy is at the same vibration as rainbows, sometimes people see them as a color or circles or waves of color.

If you want to start seeing angels, the first step is to ask your guardian angel to show you what he or she looks like, or ask for help to see your angels.

Simply pray: "My dear guardian angel, I would like to start seeing you, please help me with this."

How to practice seeing Angels.

When you want to start seeing angels, I recommend first practicing learning how to see auras. Why? Because when you do this, you get an idea of the kind of energy frequency that angels radiate at, so you have a clearer idea of what to look for.

Angel Workout

Practice this at night-time with a friend. If you don't have a friend to practice with, you can also try gazing at strangers' auras when you are out. But it is important to start doing this at night time, because auras are harder to see during the day when the sun is out. Once you get used to knowing what you are looking for, then you can practice during the day too.

You will need a candle.

Step One: Get a candle

Step Two: Play some meditation music

Step Three: Ask; "Dearest angels, I ask that you help me learn how to see you."

Step Four: Light the candle

Step Five: Close your eyes and count down from ten to one, three times. You want to be slowly becoming more and more relaxed, and when you feel your emotions and your mind calm, open your eyes.

Step Six: Gaze at the glow around the candle

By gazing I mean relax your eyes and use a soft day dreamy look steadily looking at the glow rather than an intense stare. Often with clairvoyance, you tend to see things out of the corner of your eyes or in a day-dreamy state, rather than when you are in left-brain analytical mode. The imagination is the seat of your spiritual sight. Your brow chakra which is located above your eyebrows.

If you have a friend with you, ask your friend to stand against a wall. Choose a wall that has blank walls. Look around your friend's body to see if you can see a light like the glow around the candle. If you can you are seeing your friend's aura. If you are having trouble, ask your friend to think of something that makes her or him angry or excited. Strong emotions tend to push our aura's out. Use a soft gazed focus not a stare. You want your eyes to be gazing around your friend. Start looking for angels around him or her too.

If you are alone, gaze at the candle and ask the angels to show up in your room where you are meditating. Practice looking for them. Remember they will appear very much like the glow around a candle so you might see sparks of light at first rather than an angel looking figure. Practice this exercise regularly. Especially at first. During the week ask that you see angels wherever you go. Start looking for them around people, practice in the evenings. Usually people feel or sense angels before they see them.

If you get discouraged practice visualizing or imagining different objects. People sometimes think they don't know how to visualize or how to imagine. My clients might ask: "What do you mean when I say have a mental picture?"

Everyone can visualize. Try this. Close your eyes and don't think of an orange. What do you see?

Close your eyes and think of your best friend. What does he or she look like?

Or your pet, or the table in your living room. You can visualize. You can imagine, you can get a mental picture and you can see things with your eyes closed.

Keep using your inner vision

You can use your inner vision to detect places in your body that need healing, see problems or habits in an energetic pattern, and then send them light so they will change or dissolve. You can use your inner vision to set up your intentions on the spiritual plane, so they will be easier to manifest in the physical plane, to send loved one's messages telepathically, to determine the solution to a problem, to see the spiritual perspective of a situation, to foretell the future and to read people's energy.

Practice using your inner sight every day. Start imagining you can see angels. Your higher self already knows how to see angels. So, use your imagination to help you at first. Don't discount your imagination as "making things up." Your imagination is the doorway to receiving visions and intuitive messages. Always pray: "Angels, protect me with love and light and show me what you most want me to see."

Your eyes transmit and receive energy

Your physical eyes truly are the windows to your soul. You can transmit and receive energy through your physical eyes. That is why ancient people often feared the evil eye. I am sure you have had the experience of someone giving you a dirty look. Remember how such a look made you feel? Some looks are so filled with hate or intensity you may feel as if you have received a blow to your stomach. This is what is meant by the statement "if looks could kill".

You are always unconsciously transmitting your emotions through your eyes to those around you. Once you are aware of this you can use your eyes to transmit qualities that will benefit others such as love, joy or patience.

If someone wishes you ill will for any reason, and sends you an unkind look, you can cancel out the effects simply by sending them back a stronger beam of love. When you radiate light and love and stay in your center, no one will be able to throw you off balance emotionally. You can protect your aura by imagining you are in a human hamster ball. One of those clear PVC balls that are about seven feet round. If you are an empath or lightworker, or sensitive do this often.

Angel Workout

The next time someone gives you a dirty look, practice imagining that you are sending them a beautiful beam of light from your eyes. This beam of light is a penetrating gaze of harmony and goodwill. Use your eyes consciously throughout the day to send streams of light and joy to those around you. Whenever you think of someone or something, send it a stream of light too with your inner eyes.

How to see angels with your eyes closed

Now you are going to learn how to see angels with your eyes closed using your inner eyes. Put on your favorite relaxing music. Get comfortable in a chair or lie down. Close your eyes, and let's begin.

Step One. Begin relaxing your body, allow yourself to go deeper and deeper into relaxation. Calm your mind and calm your emotions, use your breath to slow down and relax your entire body.

Step Two. Call divine light to you. Imagine your body filling with more light than it has ever held before. Feel yourself becoming lighter, and lighter, and more radiant. You are now filled with radiant white light. In your imagination, picture yourself as a radiant being of light. Let yourself relax in this state for a few moments enjoying the luxuriousness of the light.

Step Three. Now bring your attention to the mental screen in your mind. Ask your guardian angel to appear on this mental screen. Use your inner vision to see your guardian angel. You intuitively already know how to do this. Do not strain, but simply relax and allow an image of your guardian angel to form in your mind.

Step Four. Look closely at your guardian angel. Begin to describe to yourself what you see. How tall is your guardian angel? What kinds of clothing does he appear in? What color are his eyes, his hair, his skin tone? See if you can notice the energy around his body and look for any colors that you can see in his aura.

Step Five. Ask your guardian angel to help you see the other angels that are in your home. In your mind's eye, go from room to room and see if you notice other angels there. Maybe you have an angel or two hanging out in the kitchen, or by the TV or sitting on the sofa. Sometimes a couple of angels will hang out in my house sitting on the piano.

Where do you see or sense angels hanging out in your house? If you are struggling to see them, ask your inner eyes to show you where they would be if you could see them.

Step Six. Ask your guardian angel to take you to a place in the angelic realm. When you get there in your imagination, look around with your inner eyes. What can you see? Are there other angels there? Practice using your three-sixty-degree range of vision. Notice what is behind you, and what is above you. Extend your vision out further, and see if you can see into the future. What pictures and images come to you?

Step Seven. Ask the angels to show you a picture about a question you have regarding your life. Let whatever images come arise. Do not edit or censor any. Don't worry if it feels like you are making it up, or that your visions are not real – this is common. Just keep practicing and trust the process. As you become more experienced and see the results of your work, you will naturally feel more confident.

Step Eight. Now form a picture of yourself in your imagination. Ask to see what angels surround you at this time. If you like, you can darken the image of yourself so that it is almost like a silhouette. Sometimes people find it easier to see angels around themselves this way. Pay particular attention to the area around your head and shoulders – that is the most common place for angels to appear. What angels do you see with you at this time? How many are there?

Step Nine. Finally form a picture of a friend or loved one in your imagination. Ask to see what angels are with this person at this time. Use the same process as outlined in step eight. How many angels are with your friend? If you like you can ask one of the angels a question about their purpose and function.

Step Ten. When you are ready bring your attention back to this time and place. Instruct your mind that it will awaken feeling refreshed and better than before. If you feel a bit spacey have a piece of toast or wash your face with cold water. Eating root vegetables or grains is a good way to become grounded.

Angel Workout

Practice closing your eyes for a few seconds wherever you go today.

How to See Angels with Your Eyes Open

After you have practiced seeing angels with your eyes closed, and feel comfortable with the method outlined, you will be ready to begin seeing angels with your eyes open. This is a fun skill to learn because once you know how to do it, you can do it wherever you go, and you will see angels everywhere.

Before you begin to look for angels though, practice using your inner sight to scan the energy of a room, and the energy of people you come into contact with. As you get used to viewing these subtle frequencies, your ability will naturally increase.

The most important step to remember is that even though your physical eyes are open, you will still be using your inner eyes to see the angels. You may experience some physical sensations too, however, like seeing sparks of light or different colors. Many people see these things from the corner of their eyes rather than in front view.

You will see people's aura's as a radiant glow of light around their body, just like the glow from a candle flame. As your skill level improves, you will be able to discern different colors within the aura. You may start seeing angels as a shape of light too. Then you will begin to recognize more detail in the shape until you can see their features clearly. Remember, angels are made from energy that vibrates at a higher frequency than humans do, so they will not appear as solid as humans are.

Angel Workout

Relax your body. Concentrate on deepening your breathing. Take deep, slow breaths. The best time to start practicing is when you are out somewhere in a relaxed environment, like a park or a café, just relaxing and hanging out. Relax your eyes, don't strain or focus hard. Trust that you will begin seeing angels today. Say a quick prayer to the angel of inner vision who is sponsoring your growth to help you.

"Dear angel of inner vision, I ask that you help me begin to see angels with my eyes open. Thanks so much."

Choose a person to put your attention on. This can be a stranger within view or anyone nearby. Begin using the eyes of your mind to see them. You are activating your third eye center. Imagine there is an actual eye in the center of your forehead, and you can literally see with this eye. Your third eye will work in tandem with your physical eyes for this task, transmitting images back and forth so you can see the angels on your mental screen. Look around the shoulder and head area of the person you have picked, and see or sense where their angels are. What do you notice? Where can you see the angels? What do they look like? Are they large or small? Are they female or male?

If you are having trouble seeing them, ask your mind this question: If you could see them, what would they look like? Do the exercise pretending that you can see them and write down your answers in your angel journal. Your intuition is a great conduit of psychic information, and will help you. Because many people are not used to using the inner sight, it can take a while for this skill to become more familiar and feel 'real.' Just keep trusting the process. The more you practice, the better you will get, and the more confidence you will develop in your ability.

Angel Workout

Begin today to start looking for angels wherever you go. Especially look for them around people and in places of nature. Everyone has at least one angel around them – see if you can begin to spot them. Sometimes you will see them hovering around a person's head, sometimes they may be standing just next to a person, or slightly behind him or her. Some people have so many angels surrounding them, they look like they are in a fishbowl filled with angels. Small children and people who love angels are frequently surrounded by many of them.

Have fun with this exercise.

DAY SEVEN. HOW TO HEAR YOUR ANGELS

Clairaudience is a form of psychic intuition. The prefix "clair," means "clear", and the suffix "audience, means "hearing". The word reflects the psychic's ability to tune in to the energy of otherworldly realms. Clairaudients hear, rather than think, through the information they receive. Clairaudience means clear hearing.

"My dear guardian angel, I ask that I be a clear and open channel to receiving divine messages in an audible way. Please help me hear your messages and daily guidance. Help me hear both inner messages I receive, and messages I overhear. Help me practice, clear psychic hearing. Help me distinguish between angel messages, and when I think I am just making it up. And so it is, Amen"

How do you hear your angels?

There are two ways you will hear your angels talking to you.

1. Inner hearing
2. Outer hearing

Much psychic work takes place in your imagination, so yes, at first it will feel like you are making it up. That's why angels implore you to write down whatever messages they give you. *Even when you feel as if you are making it up. Write it down anyway.* The angels say "We implore you to do this for two reasons. One, if you don't, you are likely to forget the conversations we have. Two, when you write it down, there is a tangible process to putting pen to paper and you can get into the flow. You also have proof for later down the road when you see what comes to pass, and what doesn't. That is where the evidence is". Your job is to ask.

Angel workout:

Step One; Ask your angels a question you would like to know the answer to right now. Use whatever comes to mind, this is angel playtime remember, so don't judge your question. Just ask it. Ask an open-ended question, rather than a question that can be answered with a yes or no for right now. For example, "How does Peter feel about me?" "Should I take this job in Louisiana?" "Where's the remote control?"

Step Two; Get quiet. Getting quiet means you need to set aside fifteen minutes a day. Fifteen minutes is not that much time to set aside each day when you are learning a new language. You are learning the angelic language and it doesn't happen overnight. So get used to practicing if you are serious about hearing angel messages. Start taking long deep breaths, close your eyes, have a pen and paper ready to write.

Step Three; Listen. Listen to whatever comes into your mind. Then write down the answer you get as quickly as possible. Use a felt pen and a notebook, something that will glide across the paper easily. Don't try to edit what you are writing. Just Ask, Listen and Write. Free write like you would do in creative writing. You may be saying: "I am not a good writer" Being a good writer has nothing to do with it. Nor does being in the right mood to have an angel conversation.

All you need to do is set aside the same time each day for thirty days as you are doing using this workbook, and do this simple process. The angels recommend you do this either first thing in the morning, just before you are going to sleep, or set aside a quiet fifteen minutes for your angel talk. If you have a lot of noise in your house and you share a bedroom, either go sit outside or lock yourself in the toilet. The angels say they have plenty of messages they want to share with you. Give the angels an opportunity to show up and show off for you.

You will receive a lot of audible messages through clairaudience. What is clear audience? Or clear hearing? Clairaudience means the faculty of perceiving as if by hearing, what is inaudible. It comes from the

French word 'clair' meaning clear, and audience meaning 'hearing'. Clairaudience can also be called psychic hearing or inner hearing or spiritual hearing. It is hearing outside of the normal scope of awareness.

Practice receiving messages using your inner hearing, do the above exercise every day for at least thirty days. The evidence will show up as time goes by. You might ask: "Dear angels, how does Peter feel about me?" Then you free write the answer you think you are getting from your angels. "Peter loves you and is attracted to you, but he is not your true refuge, your true refuge is in your own heart, and finding safe places to create within your core during the day. He is on his own healing path too. You two will either grow closer together as you commit to your spiritual journey, and as he is pulling his life back together, or you will grow further apart over the course of this year. "You; "Well is there a future for us?"

Inner hearing free write: "Yes, dear one, the story is not finished yet. This is not the end of the chapter to this story. He will contact you within seven days."

You ask a question, you listen for an answer, you write down what you hear like when you are free writing. Keep asking questions and writing down answers for about twenty minutes. My client who did this exercise got confirmation from three different sources that week confirming that her friend would show up. The next day there was an email from a mutual friend she had not heard from in ages talking about her and her friend. The second was a dream she had where he was kissing her on her forehead, telling her not to worry about everything. The third was a song coming on the radio that was special to both of them. The guy did text her before the seven days were up, and yes, they did get together.

Another example is where one of my clients was having problems with his health. He was sick, and not getting the help he needed to get well. He asked the angels to help him find a doctor who specialized in what he needed. He heard a voice in his head saying, "Google search diabetes doctors in your area." He did. Turned out he had adult onset diabetes.

I have had this experience happen several with my health. May of 2006, I had a horrendous tummy ache on a field trip with my son Kylan, who was nine at the time. It came on suddenly, and I ended up in the ER. The doctors sent me home with a diagnosis of tummy pain, and a bottle of antibiotics and pain killers.

Twelve days later, I started seeing orange flowers coming out of my blue bedroom walls. I was concerned that I was hallucinating. It was about nine on a Saturday night. I didn't have a doctor, because I hardly ever got sick. I did not know who to call. I said "Angels, help, what do I do?" I clearly heard a voice say "doctor on call, which I proceeded to Google search. It turned out there was a mobile doctors service called Doctor on Call in Albuquerque. I called them.

Doctor Vigil arrived at my house twenty minutes later, took blood samples, and examined me. The next day he called me, and said he was coming over. He arrived at my house and said: "Catherine I think your appendix burst the day you went to the ER. You need to go to hospital - immediately."

My whole body was septic from the burst appendix. The doctors did not think I would make it out of the hospital alive. Statistically, people die within twelve to seventy-two hours from an untreated, burst appendix. I had gone nearly two weeks. I was in hospital for a month, and three surgeries later, I was released. The angels had saved my life again.

What process do I use to hear my angels?

1. Ask a question
2. Listen for an answer

This may seem simplistic. Signs that you are clairaudient or have psychic hearing abilities are: you hear buzzing or ringing in your ears a lot, you hear footsteps, creaky noises or knocking. For example, when my great uncle died, my great aunt used to hear his footsteps walking outside her bedroom window.

You hear dead people, spirit guides or your guardian angels talking to you. You talk to yourself a lot. You hear voices in your head. How do you know the difference between mental illness and clairaudience? Mediums who channel dead people, angels or spiritual guidance do this by using their clairaudient ability to hear voices in their head, it's almost like eavesdropping on a conversation in the spiritual realms. The voices are soft, gentle, and you can control when you hear them. I hear dead people, my ancestors, spirit guides and pets as well as angels. They usually have messages of love for their ones left behind.

Angel messages always come in waves of love. I hear a loving voice in my head, and sometimes when I am channeling messages for clients, it's almost like I'm the vehicle the message is coming through. My client will ask me a question, and I will be in a semi-trance state, but aware what is going on. I hear the angels tell me an answer to give them. I often say the messages come through me, not from me.

With a mental illness you may hear voices, but you may not be able to control them. You may hear voices telling you to harm yourself, or to harm someone else. Divine guidance will NEVER tell you to harm yourself, nor will your guardian angel. If you are hearing voices that frighten you, please ask your guardian angel to make those voices stop. If they persist, seek help from a trained professional.

Clairaudient messages are usually heard with your inner ear. The angels, spirit guides and dead people communicate telepathically, so that is why you hear a subtle voice inside your head. Sometimes you hear messages externally, someone might be having a conversation that you overhear that sounds like the message is meant directly for you. I hear both. How does clairaudience, clairvoyance, telepathy, clairsentience and claircognition work? Think of your body as a broadcasting station. Your energetic field is constantly broadcasting and receiving messages all day long, so is your physical body and your emotional body.

Angel Workout

How to increase your clairaudience

The first thing you need to do is practice listening. Practice listening to people when you have a conversation with someone, and practicing listening to your inner voice. Most people have their faces in their phones or their tablets half the day, and aren't listening to anything. Try tuning in rather than tuning out.

1. Practice listening with your physical ears first. Really tune in to the noises around you. Close your eyes. What can you hear? Right now I hear footsteps above me, car traffic on the road outside, someone tooted their horn, the hum of my computer, a ringing in my ears, the wind blowing, a plane overhead. What can you hear? Make a list.

2. Practice imagining sounds, a baby laughing, thunder clapping, favorite songs, fire crackling, cocoa pops popping, guitar strumming, an ambulance siren. Practice imagining sounds right inside your head. Start with a favorite song, because that's easiest. Anyone can hear Happy Birthday inside their head.

3. Listen to music. I recommend baroque, classical, jazz or anything instrumental to start off with, so you are not distracted by the words of a song. Listen to the many layers in the music, and try to differentiate between instruments. Can you hear a violin? A saxophone? A piano? A trombone? The drums? Baroque music is good because it automatically puts your brain into a state of being more psychic. I suggest staying away from ambient music or new age for the purposes of this exercise. Ambient and new age music is great to practice channeling or automatic writing with, but classical or an orchestra is best for differentiating sounds for the purposes of this exercise

4. Meditate. What is meditation? Closing your eyes and listening to your inner voice, your inner guidance, any angel messages you might be getting. I often use a two-step process where I will write down a question at night-time, and listen for an answer. I

ask: "Dearest angels, give me the information that will most help me while I sleep." When you wake up in the morning or during the night, keep a notepad by your bed and make a bullet point list of what you hear. At first it will feel like you are making it up. But remember you are learning a new language. A psychic language. So practice daily.

5. If you have a formal meditation practice that you like, keep up the practice. Insight meditation, guided meditations, and Zen meditation are all good practices, as are self-compassion and loving kindness meditations. Self-compassion meditation is especially helpful for lightworkers and empaths. You need to replenish and learn how to look after yourself when you are receiving and giving out energy. YouTube search 'self-compassion guided meditations' to find one you like.

Angel Workout

Begin listening for inner messages from your angels and practice listening deeply to words people are saying when they talk to you. Practice listening deeply.

DAY EIGHT. HOW TO FEEL ANGELS

Clairsentience means clear feeling. The prefix "clair", means "clear", and the suffix "sentience", means "feeling". The word reflects your ability to psychically feel energy. Clairsentients sense or feel, rather than think through the information they receive.

Begin to practice clairsentience today. Ask, "Dear guardian angel, I ask that you help me feel the presence of angels around me. I ask you to help me pick up other people's feelings, and tune into their energy vibration and the vibration of places I visit. Help teach me how to protect my own energy fields from being too empathetic, and absorbing other people's energy. Teach me how to feel energy without taking it on in my own energetic body."

Clairsentience is the ability to feel clearly. It is how to receive messages from the angels in your body and through your emotions.

With your spiritual sense of feeling, you can:

- Experience intuition
- Experience gut feelings or hunches
- Feel other sensations in your body that seem to give you a specific message
- Sense how things will turn out
- Feel auras
- Feel angels
- Feel the vibrations of people, places and things
- Sense a person's mood without them uttering a word

Clairsentients could be considered synonymous with empaths. An empath is someone who has high levels of empathy, 97 per cent higher than the average human. Empathy is the ability to understand and share the feelings of another person.

An empath is someone with the psychic ability to perceive the mental or emotional state of another person. For the purposes of this chapter I will use clairsentients and empaths as one and the same.

How do you feel energy?

What do I mean when I say "feel energy"? Have you ever had the experience of meeting someone for the first time and got a weird feeling in the pit of your stomach? Have you ever felt pins and needles or chills down the side of your arms or behind your neck when you've walked into a room, or someone has said something to you? If so, these are examples of spiritual sensing. Our spiritual senses work in tandem with our physical senses, so if you want to improve your ability to be clairsentient, you must practice your ability to feel things in the physical too.

If you have never felt "psychic chills" a sensation like pins and needles running down your arms, or anxiety in your chest when someone says something uncanny, or any of the above examples, let me give you a couple more examples you might relate to. When you go to a birthday party, a wedding or a place where there is a celebration going on, there's usually a lot of joy, right? You feel that joy and participate in it by laughing and joking and enjoying the company of the people around you. That is one way you are experiencing energy on a physical level. The energy of joy is present.

If you go to a funeral where people are grieving, and everyone is sad, crying, or in shock, you feel sadness too right? You are picking up the energy of the room, and the group, as well as your own sadness. The energy of everyone else's emotions, as well as yours, amplifies the energy of sadness ten-fold.

If someone gives you a dirty look, you may feel angry, scared or intimidated, depending on your mood and personality. The way you feel when someone gives you a dirty look is a good example of clairsentience, because they are not speaking any words, but their look says it all. It is the same as when someone glares at you, or when someone who is in love with you gazes deeply into your eyes, you feel their emotion.

When babies are pre-verbal, mothers often sense what they need. When men are having affairs and wives suspect, this comes from intuition. Per studies, 85 per cent of women who have a nagging feeling that their husband or boyfriend are cheating on them, turn out to be right. Sorry guys, the statistics are not the same for you. Why this happens when it comes to affairs, I truly don't know. But we all have intuition whatever gender you are.

Intuition is not a magical power. It is real, and scientific studies show how the brain chemistry and subconscious mind work with the conscious mind and exhibit different physical symptoms in your body. You can learn how to feel the presence of angels just as you feel the presence or energy of someone giving you an angry look.

All emotions carry energy, all objects carry energy, everything that exists in this physical world is made up of energy. That is a scientific fact. It makes sense that you can feel energy. You are feeling energy all day long. The temperament of your boss at work, the mood at happy hour on a Friday, the energy in a cinema room at the end of a very sad movie, for example. All day long you are picking up energy from other people and sending out energy of your own.

We are all mini-sensory stations receiving and broadcasting energy all day (and night) long. At night, you may receive even more clairsentient messages. Some people experience flashbacks and panic attacks at night-time more frequently than during the day. Our bodies are highly tuned frequency detectors, and every emotion has a different frequency vibration. Think of the frequency of joy, the frequency of depression, the frequency of bitterness, the frequency of rage. It takes energy to carry those emotions in your body.

To become more clairsentient or empathetic, you simply practice tuning in to the energy of:

One, what emotion you are carrying right now

Two, what emotion other people are expressing

Three, how other peoples' emotions affect yours

Four, what the vibe of a room is like when you first walk into it

Pay attention, and be mindful during the day of what you are experiencing physically, and what you are experiencing each moment of the day.

Angel workout

For the rest of this week I want you to:

Pay attention to any messages your body seems to be giving you about a person or a situation. What kind of body signals do you get?

See if you can feel the energy of a room when you walk into it. Do this everywhere you go - shops, restaurants, parties, casinos, bars, graveyards, your best friend's house.

See if you can gauge what someone's mood is before they begin talking to you.

Pay attention to your intuition. What message is your intuition giving you today?

People who are highly empathetic pick up 97 percent more messages than the average person. I am one of those people, for me, it is hard to understand what it is like to not pick up messages. People who are sociopaths or psychopaths don't have the ability to feel other people's emotions, they lack empathy and they lack remorse. They genuinely are not capable of feeling what you are feeling.

When you are highly empathetic, it can be exhausting, so you must learn how to modulate your empathy to prevent empathy fatigue(more in later chapters). If I go to a casino, I get sensory overload that feels like being jolted with intense electricity currents.

Old bars can carry a lot of draining, murky energy too – it's exhausting for empaths to be around alcoholics and addicts, or even people who are constantly complaining or are very excitable. At bars and strip clubs, the energy can be intolerable, because it's such a low energy vibration. Plus a lot of dead addicts and alcoholics hang out in those places, trying to get their fix through the people who are drinking in bars or attending strip clubs.

Many bars carry low energy, however there can be places where people drink that are quite jovial and jocular. It is up to you to determine how much energy you can handle. There is a big difference in the energy of a professional burlesque show in New Orleans or Las Vegas, for example, than a seedy strip club in a red light district

What can be crazy making, is when children pick up things intuitively, and are told by parents that it's not real; or when you have a persistent nagging feeling your partner is cheating on you, and you get accused of being jealous or insecure. People lie. You can lie to a psychic or empath, but as psychics (and empaths) become accustomed to tuning into the messages they are getting, they trust their bullshit detector more. You will too, the more you practice.

What does angel energy feel like?

Angels vibrate at a higher frequency than humans so their energy is finer. That said, they can feel as real as a person standing beside you. As I mentioned earlier, I have literally had angels hit me over the head with a piece of four by two. It is important you get a sense of what different energy feels like, which is why we have spent a lot of time today talking about how you pick up psychic messages on both a physical and non-physical level.

Angel energy comes when you ask it to. It also comes when angels want to send you a warning signal and alarm bell. Let me give you an example of a warning. One client of mine had a love interest who had a very bad drug problem. She was so intoxicated by love, she could not see him clearly. For his part, he had a vested interest in keeping her interested, so he could resource her. He knew how to play her. Which is not to say there were not valid feelings between them, but the whole situation was direly dangerous and toxic. I have yet to meet anyone who has walked away from a relationship with a hardcore addict and gone: "Wow, that was a ton of fun."

My client came to a point where she could see how this person was manipulating her, and she felt worse after seeing him not better. Often she was exhausted after seeing him, and it would take her two days to get back on track. She was at the point where she loved him, but she was ready to walk away. She had no contact with him for a couple of months. One day, when she needed a temporary roommate, she had the idea to email him and see if he could stay for a week.

"No, no, no!" screamed her guardian angels. My client was at the point where she was starting to put those rose-colored glasses back on and think: "Oh, it wouldn't be that bad him coming to stay." Within twenty-four hours her angels swung into action big time. Friends of hers on the other side of the world could feel a sense of danger around her. The morning after she had emailed her ex-boyfriend, there was an email from a psychic friend in another country saying: "I don't want to scare you but I've been getting signs you are in danger." One of her friends she had lunch with that day said "_____, I had a bad feeling last night. You contacted_____, Nothing good is going to come of it. Please tell me it wasn't true. He's dangerous, he is consumed by his addiction, he traumatizes you." The third sign was that for the next twenty-four hours, she too felt anxiety in the pit of her stomach when thinking of what she had requested. Everywhere she went she saw signs of "going down the rabbit hole like Alice", which was her term for him falling prey to the craziness of his addiction.

My client listened to the concerns her trusted friends were feeling. She listened to the emotions when she thought about the reality of what his presence would bring. Within twenty-four hours she sent him an email that said she didn't want him around her at all. Immediately, she said, she felt like a weight had lifted.

When she awoke the next morning, there was a new email in her inbox from a friend saying: "Your angels love you so much, they jumped into action as soon as they feared for your safety and well-being, see how many people they used to pass on their frantic messages of concern." This was confirmation she had done the right thing.

Other ways clients have felt their angels energy is like waves of bliss flowing over them.

There are many ways you can feel your angels, but it's important to be able to sense energy first.

Angel workout for today:

How to feel your guardian angels presence

Step one. Begin by requesting: "My dear guardian angels, I invite your energy more fully into my life, help me feel the waves of energy you are broadcasting to me, help me tune into your frequencies, help me pay attention to the messages I receive in my body, help me to discern the vibes I am getting around me. Most importantly teach me to feel the difference between which ones come from heavenly assistance, and which ones come from my own personality, and so it is, Amen."

Step two. Imagine your guardian angel cradling you at night when you go to sleep. This angel is seven feet tall with huge wings, and you can rest in her/his arms and feel her/his breath on your cheek. I have had clients who have felt angels breath, and felt their hair being stroked gently, or their back being softly caressed. I have had the experience of angels putting their hands on my body and doing angel reiki on me at night time when I've been sick. I have felt angels on either side of me at different times. I remember feeling three angels in a house in 2010, they were in the kitchen with me. "We're real Catherine," they said. "We do actually exist, you know."

How do you know the difference between psychosis and actual angel messages? The evidence is always in what shows up. Angel messages will never tell you to harm someone or yourself. They think we are way too hard on ourselves. Ask to feel them, then make notes of how and when you felt their presence throughout the day.

Step three. Do an invocation to your guardian angels, and use all of your senses to feel them – your sight, your smell, your hearing and your psychic empathy. Say: "I now invoke a circle of loving angels around me, Raphael before me, Gabriel behind me, Michael at my right and Uriel at my left. My guardian angel beside me, my angel guide above me and my birth angel below me to guide my feet."

Invoke any angels you feel comfortable with. In your imagination, build up this astral impression of the angels as strongly as you can, see them as vividly as you can see your best friends, get a sense of which angel carries what energy. Get a feel for their energy.

Go through your entire day imagining you can feel angels everywhere.

Make a note here of what you experienced (yes, even if you feel like you are making it up. Just write it down anyway).

DAY NINE. HOW TO CHANNEL ANGELS

Channeling is easy. How do I know? Because I've been doing it myself for years. It is not a 'special, unique' gift that only some people get to do. It's a skill that we all possess which we can practice and develop over time. It does require more practice than other methods of communication though, and some people are definitely more naturally attuned to channeling than others. But everyone can channel their guardian angel and their higher self or inner divine being. By the end of this chapter I promise you, you will be beginning to channel.

Let me start by asking you some questions.

1. Why would you like to channel?
2. What kind of experiences have you had with channeling before?
3. Do you have any fears or concerns about channeling?
4. If yes, what are they?

The most common fear is "I won't be able to do it". This is normal, and it is also not true, so give yourself permission that by the end of this book you will be channeling your guardian angel. Another fear is "what if I channel a dark entity?" Don't worry. We are calling on angels of light and we are asking archangel Michael who is the bodyguard angel for protection. You are not going to the realm of darkness. You are going to a realm of higher conscious, a dimension where only love and light exist. You will be making an ascension, and asking for only your guardian angel to come through. Later you may practice using the same techniques to channel other angels, your angel guide, your spirit guides and any ascended beings of light that you wish. You can also use these techniques to channel messages from loved ones who have passed over. Always ask their permission first.

I channel many beings, and I channel other people's angels. I have a personal angel who I channel for only myself. I channel Angelica, who came to me when I was in New Zealand having surgery in February of 2010, and asked me to channel her. She is the female partner of Orion, who many people are channeling. Once I channeled a drunk Scottish woman. She had some great information, but I threw up afterwards, which wasn't much fun. I have also done group channelings with an individual message for everyone. One night I did a group channeling for over forty people. Everyone got an individual message. I was exhausted.

It is best to channel before eating, but have a snack so that you will be hungry while you are channeling. Don't channel after a large meal. Food is very grounding. It is great to eat after channeling, and to drink lots of water too. I also wash my hands after each client I channel for. Notice what physical sensations happen to you. You may feel very warm or very cold after a channeling session. These are simply things to be aware of and write in your journal.

Now for the fun stuff, let the channeling begin.

Firstly, we will begin by opening your chakras. Imagine your guardian angel is using a pendulum to open your crown chakra where you receive divine information like a funnel. Your angel opens your brow chakra which is your third eye and great for clairvoyance. He or she opens your ear chakras so you can hear things with clairaudience. He opens your throat chakra so you will be able to communicate verbally messages your guardian angel has for you. She opens your heart chakra so your heart will be wide open to receiving messages from your angels.

You can use this at home anytime. All you need is a pendulum. If you don't own a pendulum, don't worry, because you can visualize your chakras being opened. Just imagine your guardian angel holding a pendulum above each of the chakras, starting with the crown. A drop of tiger balm massaged into your third eye is also another useful tool, but not necessary to channel. The first most important thing to remember is that when you channel, you want to be in a relaxed comfortable, day-dreamy state of mind. This is not the time for concentrating, it is the time for letting go and being open and ready to receive.

Start with a prayer.

"Dear archangel Michael I ask you to surround me with a circle of angels for protection and that the information I most need today will come to me."

"I invite my guardian angel to use me as a conduit for divine information, and ask that I channel your messages easily and effortlessly with an open heart and open mind."

Don't worry if it feels like you are making this up. Everyone feels like this at first. It is normal and part of the process. Now we will proceed with a guided meditation to get you into a relaxed state of mind. Count backwards from ten down to one. Once you reach one, you will be completely relaxed. I will guide you to soul link with your guardian angel going up a luminous staircase to the angelic realm where the angels who are closest to earth reside.

Now you are ready to begin channeling. We will begin with a mental conversation first. I will ask you questions and you can answer them in your mind. When you have received the answer, move onto the next question. It can be helpful to hold your thumb and second finger together with your arms open, and resting gently on your lap. Make sure that both your arms and legs are uncrossed, as this is a position of receptiveness.

Your soul is always linked with your guardian angel. The first step is to link your crown chakra to your guardian angel, so you can begin downloading information from the Angel Ethernet. Do this by imagining your guardian angel above you pouring divine light into the top of your head and hooking you up to the angel internet. This is where you can start channeling your guardian angel. Think of the Angel Ethernet and channeling like your internet connection to the angel realm.

Here are some questions to begin asking your guardian angel in your mind.

What is your name? Go with the first name that pops into your head. Don't worry how bizarre it may seem, it may take several times to get a name.

Ask your guardian angel what three things he or she will bring you during the week to let you know they are real.

What are these three things?

Ask your guardian angel to make the connection between you as close as possible, so you can receive messages easily and effortlessly.

Begin asking questions:

You can ask any questions from what is my soul's purpose, to:

How can I make more money?

What foods are best for my body?

Is there a new lover coming into my life?

Remember these questions are for you and your guardian angel, and only you and your guardian angel need to know the answers. You can reveal the answers to others if you choose to

How to verbally channel other people's angels

Close your eyes and begin to breathe deeper and deeper, count backwards from ten to one.

Ask to speak to the guardian angel of _____. Use this practice ethically and only do it if someone wants you to channel their angel. I begin each channeling session by asking "dear angels, may the information that will best serve_____ come through me for the highest good of all involved. May I be a clear and open channel for divine messages." Then start to channel by asking questions out loud.

You can ask questions like:

Greetings guardian angel of _____ will you tell us your name?

What is your message for _____ today?

Here are some examples of more questions you may like to ask:

Use these questions for channeling your own guardian angel and to channel your friends. These are prompts you can ask what information you wish to know for yourself.

What is _____ life's purpose?

What is the lesson _____(name of person) is in my life to teach me?

How can I best deal with_____?

How can I become more abundant and prosperous?

How can I attract more money?

How can I attract more love?

You can also soul link to your future self, and ask your guardian angel to help you step through the doorway into the path of your highest good.

What steps do I need to take to get from where I am right now, to this possible future?

Remember, you have an inner guidance system and a divine guidance system. They work in perfect tandem with each other for your highest good. Your angel guide will help you with divine guidance and your intuition and your psychic senses are your inner guidance system. Your guardian angel will help link divine guidance to your intuition.

DAY TEN. HOW TO WRITE LETTERS TO ANGELS

Writing letters to your angels is fun and easy, and getting replies from them is even more fun. The term ghost writer is literally true in this case, although it would probably be more accurate to say angel writer. When I write books (and I know other authors who do this too, like Wayne Dyer) I literally imagine the book already exists in the spiritual plane. I see it in my mind, and as I write, I feel like I am more of a scribe writing down information that the angels are writing through me. For example, as I started writing this morning, I prayed "angels of writing, help me with writing this chapter today, and use me as a clear and open channel for the information you want to get across."

You can also use this technique for writing fiction. I like to write romance, and I can see the characters in my imagination. They come more to life the more I listen to them or observe them or write about them. Tom Cruise uses a similar process to get into character for his movies. In one interview, he said he kept a diary as part of the character he was going to play for his next movie, doing this each day for about three months before shooting would begin. He wrote in the diary as the first person of the character he was playing for three months.

Today, you are going to learn how to write to the angels, and how they can write back to you. To write a letter to them isn't hard. You can simply write a letter in a word processing program, or with a pencil or pen. Learning the process of the angels writing back to you is not much more difficult either. People have been using it for centuries. It's called automatic writing, and began as a parlor game in the latter part of the nineteenth century, gaining in popularity in the first part of the twentieth century.

William Butler Yeats was a famous writer who used automatic writing to write his poems, and everyone knows the story of Michelangelo sculpting the famous statue "David", where Michelangelo said it was simply his job to bring forth the art form that already existed. Many artists and writers feel this way. Some admit to channeling their work. Most recently authors Jerry and Esther Hicks channeled Abraham. I think most people who write or paint get into an altered state while working. While they may not call it channeling, it is an experience like meditating and getting lost in a different world where there is no time or space, and you are having a spiritual experience with your work in some way. It's no accident that ghostwriter is the word used to describe a professional writer who is hired to help someone write a book.

Now you know a little bit about the background of automatic writing, use this journal to write your first angel letter. With the start of your first meeting, take it as seriously as going to a business meeting. Set aside some quiet time, and don't write when you are drunk or using drugs. While some cultures advocate the use of drugs to put you in an altered state, you are more vulnerable to opening yourself up to negative energy when you are drunk. Meditating or listening to alpha wave music available free on YouTube will put you in a relaxed state of mind that is safer and more effective.

You can also have a warm bath to relax you first, if you like. I suggest doing this exercise at a time when you are not stressed out, ill or angry, to get the best results - especially when you first begin. And don't worry if it takes a few sessions to get going either. Like any skill, automatic writing is one that takes practice to learn. Some people pick it up straight away, and some people it takes a little longer. Just keep practicing, and as always, don't try too hard. Just listen and write down what you think you hear.

Angel Workout

Start with a prayer: "I ask the angels to provide a circle of love and light around me as I write."

Write your letter. For example: Dear angels. Or you can address it to a specific angel: My dear guardian angel, or to angels of something in particular, like Dear angels of clairvoyance. Then continue writing the letter, write whatever you like, whatever you need help with and whatever you would like to know or request.

For example, if you are having financial problems:

Dear angels of prosperity,

Help. I need to pay my car insurance, and I'm worried I'm not going to have money to pay for it.

Or dear angels what can I do about?

Do a free write without editing just like timed free writings you do in English classes. Make it about seven to fifteen minutes for the first time. Write down what you "hear". Imagine you are a scribe and the messages are coming from the angels who are using your hands to write or type the message.

Use automatic writing to practice receiving messages from you angels especially if you like to write. By practicing the tools of channeling, writing messages and using your psychic senses you will find methods that are most effective for you. You have many tools to use to talk to your angels.

Angel Workout

Write a letter to your guardian angel today. Then write a letter to yourself from your guardian angel.

Start it: "Dear_____(your name). This is your guardian angel. I have many messages to give you. Today I would like you to know:

Put a timer on for ten minutes. Google search an online countdown timer if you don't have one. You can use it directly from your phone or computer. Now free write for ten minutes a letter to yourself from your guardian angel as outlined above. When I automatic write, I put on alpha wave music from YouTube first.

DAY ELEVEN. ANGEL MAGIC FOR LOVE AND ROMANCE

One of the most requests I get is: how do you do love magic? Or can I help someone bring back a lost lover? And the most frequent psychic readings and life coaching sessions I did revolved around love and relationships. This is no surprise, say the angels. The heart rules the body. Scientists are discovering the heart has its own brain. The emotions we carry in our hearts desires can powerfully affect how we feel about ourselves, and what we manifest. Our physical heart has a brain that helps it make decisions, and our physical heart pumps healthy, life-giving blood to each of our thirty-six trillion cells all day long.

Our heart is always pumping without us having to make it pump. Just as our mind is always thinking without us having to make it think. But the energy or current we carry through our emotions and thought waves can make a huge impact on our lives. Have you ever seen someone over fifty who has an extremely bitter look on their face? Usually this means the primary emotion this person has carried throughout her life is bitterness or resentment. Whereas older people who have kind, serene faces have generally carried the emotional currents of joy or optimism.

We can choose each day what emotional currents we wish to carry, and we can change our emotional state by two ways:

1. What we choose to focus on mentally
2. Changing our physiology

What do you focus on mentally?

What you think about matters. Your thought waves will literally materialize as solid matter into your life. Does this mean when something bad happens, you have attracted it? No, because sometimes traumatic things happen. That does not mean your thoughts caused it. However, what you think about primarily, and where you put your mental focus, is very important to your health and wellbeing.

You can turn your life around in twenty-one days by consciously choosing a new thought pattern. For example, when I was a teenager I had an eating disorder. When I was twenty-two I made a conscious decision to not have an eating disorder, and I created new thought patterns for what I thought someone who had a healthy relationship with food and their body would have. I made a mental template, then wrote it down on a piece of paper. I practiced living, thinking and acting as someone who did not have an eating disorder, but someone who ate healthy food, enjoyed exercising and liked their body. Within a year my eating disorder was gone for good, and that was nearly thirty years ago.

You can change anything that you don't like in your life by changing the way you think about it. The most important rule in any magic is to remember all magic begins in the mind. Your imagination is the door way to the spiritual world, the creative realms and the inventive realms. You can use your mind to create novels, books, business plans, food plans and to bring love to you.

Make up your mind you will always attract love wherever you go

There are two secrets to attracting love and practicing love magic. Start thinking and acting as if:

1. You will always attract love wherever you go
2. The kind of guy/girl you are seeking is also seeking you

3. You may yearn for a certain person, but that person may not be for your greatest and highest good

4. When doing, love magic always ask the universe for this or something better

5. Allow the universe to bring you love in unexpected ways

6. Your job is to ask, and the angels will align the love energy and create opportunities to meet the perfect person for you

7. Don't worry about HOW it is going to happen, trust that the universe and the angels have got this

8. Don't cheat, you don't want that kind of murky, deceitful energy in your life

9. Never manipulate someone into loving you. You can request that someone return into your life for the highest good of all, but never pay a psychic who promises to reunite lovers

10. Create a vision of the kind of love you want, whether it is romantic, joyous, or passionate, and create the kind of lover you want to have

You will always meet your soul mates

There is no way you can't meet your soulmates. You have more than one soulmate, there are soul friends, soul tribes, soul families and variations of soul love. I have had soulmates turn up on my doorsteps unannounced. Your soul recognizes and blends with this person's energy. So don't worry that you have to go hunting for your soulmate, you don't. You just have to be open to the idea that the angels and the universe will create the perfect meeting for the two of you.

Twin Flames and Soul Mates

Twin Flames are spiritual twins. We only have one twin flame. You will know when you meet your twin flame. It is like meeting a part of yourself, you instantly recognize each other. You may not realize you are twin flames. There is a strong sense of recognition and your soul energy blends well together. The angels said to make this day eleven for two reasons. One, two of cups in the tarot symbolizes new romance and two in the major arcana is the high priestess, so we are combining the energy of romance, new beginnings and intuition.

Twin Flames are your spiritual identical twin. Sometimes one twin may decide to stay on the other side during a lifetime and help you from heaven. Alternatively you may have an agreement that one of you will incarnate earlier than the other twin depending on your souls' purpose. Sometimes twin flames marry and have a lifetime together. Soul mates and twin flames are often misunderstood, these topics deserve an entire book not just a day.

New Moon Intentions and Angel Magic

Setting your intentions for the month at the start of the new moon, or the start of the calendar month, is a great way to set the tone for each month and put energy into motion and plans into action. The time between the new moon and the full moon is the time of new energy growth and for lighting candles for things you want to bring into your life. The time between the full moon and the dark moon is the time for letting things go.

Choose a candle in a color you like. You can choose a candle in the color of the aura of the archangel you want to call on. You will learn the archangels' qualities and names later in this book. But for now, get a candle that you like the color of. Or if you want a good angel for manifesting, call on Zafkiel or Zadkiel, or to manifest love, call on Haniel or Chamuel or Michael.

Write a list of five things you would like to either change, have, be or do for this month. Keep your list to five or six things. I find if I make long lists, I don't stick to them, plus your energy gets diluted all over the place. So, no more than five or six things. For example, my goals for this month are to; finish this book, write 2000 words each day, strengthen my back by doing yoga each morning, strengthen my ankle by practicing the exercises each day my physiotherapist gives me, and meditate three times a day for fifteen minutes.

When I know which direction I'm headed, it gives my life more purpose and meaning. Right now, I am working hard to manifest a life-long dream, so each month my intentions reflect that. Write down the intentions you want to manifest or set in action this month:

Light your candle and meditate on the flame for fifteen minutes. Do this in the evening of either the new moon, or the start of your calendar month. I like using either tea lights, because they are small and burn quickly, or seven-day Roman Catholic candles, because you can leave them lit for seven days. You can also get guardian angel candles. Ask your guardian angel to help you with your list each day for the next month.

You can also call on specific archangels or angels from the seventy-two angels who you will meet soon. Say a prayer: *"Dear angels (or specific angels or archangels), please bless this list with light and love, lead me to the people, places and opportunities that will best help me this month. Help me manifest the items and qualities on this list, and bless it with divine love and divine light, for the highest good of all, and so it is, Amen."*

Sometimes people tell me their religion says it's wrong to pray to angels. When I use the word prayer, I mean it as the definition of politely asking for a request or petition. But do what makes you feel comfortable within your own faith.

Full Moon Gypsy Love Spell:

This spell was given to me by my dear gypsy friend, Sheena. Sheena was raised in a gypsy vardo in Ireland. I met her doing psychic readings at her fortune telling booth in Auckland, New Zealand. Sheena quickly became a soul sister, she named us "the dodge sisters" and we had many psychic adventures.

Get a candle before the next full moon. Choose one the same way as outlined above. On the full moon, light the candle and chant:

"Pray to the moon while she is round, Love for me shall now abound, on the sea and on the ground, the love I seek shall now be found."

Chant three times while gazing at the full moon. Make circles with your arms as you chant that get larger and larger.

Then chant "Oh moon I pray, bring me the love I seek today." Light the candle and leave it lit until it has burned. Love spells are good to do on Friday's since Friday is ruled by Venus, on the new moon or full moon but not during the waning moon.

That is Sheena's gypsy love spell that has worked well for me on several occasions, as well as for clients and friends.

Your Angel Workout:

What would you most like the angels to help you with in your love life starting today?

Make a list below:

Get a pink candle to represent soul love, ask the angels to bless it with love and light and to strengthen the relationship's you have, to bring you the love you seek and any other requests about love you might have. Say "dear angels, bless this candle with love and light for the highest good of all." Light, it and burn it imagining the love requests you made are being handed over to the romance angels or the angels of divine love. Know that your requests have been sent out to the angelic realm and wait and see what shows up. Usually something will show up in a month or sooner. If you are asking for love from a specific person make sure you request "this or something better"

By asking for the highest outcome or something better you are not manipulating someone into loving you and you are allowing the universe to bring you the love you seek that is for your highest good. Who you think may be a great partner may not be. The angels can find someone who is a perfect match for you. Be open to receiving love. Notice if you are extremely attached to receiving love from a particular person who may have dumped you, or may not seem that interested or who gives you mixed messages. If this is the case ask yourself if it is love you want or validation from an external source. Ask the angels to help you understand why you are seeking to be loved by this person.

You can use this exercise for someone you are attracted to. Always end it with "this or someone better." Sometimes it is the qualities we like about a person that attracts us to them. Focus on the qualities and character values of a person you would like to be with.

Imagine the universe will arrange an opportunity for you to meet the most perfect soulmate or companion for you.

Your job is to ask, and follow the inner promptings you get. The angels will work behind the scenes to arrange a meeting.

DAY TWELVE. ARE YOU AN EARTH ANGEL?

What is an earth angel? Chances are, if you bought this book, you are an earth angel, a lightworker, an empath or an angel lover.

An empath is someone who experiences or picks up on the psychological experiences, feelings, thoughts and attitudes of another person or object. Empathy is where you literally feel the feelings someone else is experiencing. It comes from the Greek word empatheia (circa 1900) em – meaning "in" and "patheia" meaning feeling or pathos. In older dictionaries an empath was named an empathist. Nowadays, we simply refer to them as empaths.

The difference between empathy and sympathy is empathy is where you put yourself in the shoes of the other person and feel what they experience. Sympathy is feeling compassion, sorrow, pity or a sense of kinship for what the person is experiencing without taking those feelings on yourself.

How to tell if you are an empath

- You pick up on the feelings of others easily
- You often feel the pain of others
- You get drained after being around some people for too long
- You get overwhelmed being in a crowd of people for too long
- Being around certain people makes you feel sick or exhausted
- You feel the vibe of a room or a person immediately
- People come to you when they have a problem
- You feel physically ill when seeing violent or horrific images in the media

- You take care of others more than you take care of yourself sometimes, putting their needs before your own
- You feel a need to be around water

Being extremely empathetic can be exhausting, but there are ways to cope that we will cover in the next chapter. You run the risk of developing empathy fatigue and must take steps to prevent it.

Earth angels:

Earth Angels are incredibly kind. They are angels from the angelic realm who have signed up to come to this planet to help humanity. They are angels who inhabit human bodies. Have you ever heard a story of where "someone showed up and helped, and was just like an angel".

Sometimes earth angels may just show up for a short time if you are in a crisis. Some earth angels have made a commitment to be on this planet for the span of a human life time. It is weird for angels to be in human bodies, because the earthy realm is much denser than the angelic realm. Some angels enjoy coming down to earth because activities like sports, showering, and eating are different here, and they enjoy an earthly experience.

People can act as earth angels, sometimes over the course of a lifetime, or just for a day. I am thinking now of driving back from Arizona to New Mexico when my kids were little. My then husband took a wrong turn in Tucson. He was grumbling that it was going to take us longer to get home. I wasn't feeling particularly happy about having to take back roads either, but it would have been more hassle to turn around and back track to get to a main road. So I said: "Maybe the angels wanted us to come this way."

There was a little bit more grumbling, but then we all settled down to enjoy the "scenic" route we were taking in the middle of nowhere. About two hours into our journey, we spotted a car that had overturned, and a couple standing a few feet away from it. The couple had been there for about six hours, praying someone would drive by (this was really in the backwaters, there were no global positioning systems or cell phone reception.) Their car had completely flipped over, and it was a miracle they were still standing. We gave them a ride to the nearest town, which was another two hours away, and got them to the hospital.

Sometimes you may find yourself in situations where you act as an angel for other people.

Angel Workout

Have you ever had an experience where you felt like an earth angel?

Have you ever had an experience when someone acted like an earth angel for you? Write a paragraph about it here:

What experience of empathy stands out most strongly in your mind?

Lightworkers, empaths and other highly sensitive, intuitive or psychic people

Lightworkers came to this earth to bring more light, love and healing to the planet. All earth angels are lightworkers by default, but not all lightworkers are earth angels.

Lightworkers tend to like being in the light, they are very empathetic, which means they pick up other people's feelings and energy easily. They can be accused of being "overly sensitive" when in fact, they are highly intuitive, and can tune into other people's emotions easily.

Sometimes lightworkers put other people's needs before their own. And when I say lightworker, please note I am also including empaths, psychics and highly intuitive people in this group.

Empaths have the ability to tune into what people are feeling, they pick up feelings, they are very clairsentient, and often don't know how to block other people's energy, so can feel drained quite easily.

Psychics have highly developed intuitive abilities. I've been psychic since I was born; I don't know what it's like to not be psychic. There are different types of psychics, pet psychics, psychics who are good at locating lost items, people who get strong psychic imprints from holding objects, can talk to dead people, or get visions of the future.

For a long time I didn't want to think of myself as psychic, because I did not want to think I had a special gift. My friend Yancey, who is a gifted psychic reader, said she believes being psychic is a gift that not everyone is born with. I believe that everyone has the ability to learn how to be more psychic, but some people are born naturally with second sight. My grandmother, being the seventh daughter of a seventh daughter, was highly clairvoyant, and read tea leaves and cards. Psychic people can be at risk for taking on too much of other people's energy. Professional psychics, also, have to be careful to practice good self-care, and have strong boundaries so as to not burn out.

The traits that empathetic people have can put them at risk for being targets for emotional predators. It's important for empathetic people to know this. Sandra L Brown, who specializes in treating women with PTSD from relationships with sociopaths and dangerous men, has done studies in this area. The women studied were 97 percent more empathetic than a regular person. Sandra said while she suspected emotional predators target empathetic, kind people, she had no idea how far off the Richter scale it would be in terms of the level of empathy. Empathetic people need to pay close attention, and here are some traits that can put you at risk.

1. A high level of empathy
2. High tolerance to neglect
3. Blind trust
4. Insane loyalty

5. Falling in love with potential
6. Putting others needs before your own
7. Having sex early on in a relationship

What kind of people should empaths be especially aware of:

- Addicts
- Sociopaths
- People with a lot of nervous energy
- People who take up a lot of time
- People who have high levels of energy

Sociopaths are tricky because they deliberately target empathetic people. They are good at observing what you need and resourcing you. You may not know how to recognize a sociopath. They are extremely manipulative and pathological liars. They often hook people in with a sympathy story or by love bombing you. They will keep you up late at night when you first meet and want to have a lot of sex. This does two things: the lack of sleep makes your judgement less clear and sex releases oxytocin in women the love bonding hormone. You may feel as if you are falling in love and it may feel intoxicating. This too gives you poor judgement.

It is very important for empathetic people to not sleep with someone until you have dated for a couple of months. And to limit dates to three times a week for the first six weeks. This way you will stay grounded and can see if actions match words. Studies done by Dr Sandra L Brown show empathetic people are the most at risk to dangerous men, sociopaths and emotional predators.

To Learn More:

Visit Sandra's website at saferelationshipsmagazine.com
Read Emotional Vampires by Bernstein
Or How to spot a dangerous man by Sandra Brown

Empaths, kind hearted people and lightworkers must learn about manipulative people and how they manipulate because empaths are the most at risk.

Addicts too are extremely manipulative and crazy making. If you are highly empathetic do not try to help addicts. Leave that for trained professionals. The most you will get from an addict is nothing. You can pray for friends with addiction problems. But hanging around addicts puts you at risk for being resourced and emotionally depleted. Empathetic people need to take stronger precautions than regular people. I can't stress this enough. Your kind heartedness can be a doorway to danger.

If there are people who drain you that you no longer want in your life, simply raise your vibration. They will drop away instantly. Remember, you are not doing anyone a favor for being a listening board to their complaints. These people are not your friends. They are emotional vampires who drain your energy, so they leave feeling great, and you're left feeling exhausted. Unless you are a paid professional, do not let anyone do this to you.

There is a big difference between a friend who is going through a crisis, and friends who are constantly complaining and criticizing. Do both of you a favor. Raise your vibration and they will automatically drop away. I see it happen every day. It's like you are tuning into a different radio station, the station that plays happy songs, not the station that plays sad love songs. You will feel more energized, and be able to broadcast more love and light to the world, and the constant complainers will gently leave your life. Don't worry, they will find someone else to complain too.

I used to have a friend who would bribe his way into my home. He would bring a bottle of vitamin water. I was "allowed" five minutes of speaking time. Then the conversation would immediately turn to him, and he would spend the next hour complaining, or wanting me to give him a free reading. I would always be exhausted after he left.

Watch and see if people's actions match their words. That is the quickest way to learn about them. You must do this for at least three months.

To wash away psychic or emotional debris you have picked up buy a bar of soap from the Dead Sea. One with Nature makes these, and they come in many different fragrances. They are great. They work on three levels.

On the physical level, when you wash with the soap the salt scrubs away dead skin cells. The Dead Sea has the most concentrated form of salt and minerals than any other ocean in the world. The salt is absorbed into your body via your epidermis. After about three days, you may taste a salty feeling in your mouth.

On the emotional level, it clears away any emotional debris you may have picked up during the day. And on the psychic level, if anyone is sending you challenging energy, the salt automatically deflects that energy to where it belongs. If you are a counselor, a teacher, an earth angel, a psychic reader, or a nurse, you must use this soap. The results are amazing.

Lastly, if you find yourself crying over someone, cry onto a picture of them. These are angel tears, and they are toxic to the person who has hurt you. This is not meant to harm them, simply to send the energy back to where it belongs.

Angel Workout

Make a list of the people you spend the most time with. Pay attention during the week to who enhances your life and who drains it. Notice where your energy is going. Is this where you want to put your time and resources? Your time and resources are valuable. Where do you most want to put your time and resources? What changes can you make to do this?

DAY THIRTEEN. THE ANGELS AND POST TRAUMATIC STRESS

What is post-traumatic stress?

Post-Traumatic Stress is a condition that is triggered by a terrifying event. You can get it by either experiencing the event, or being a witness. Events that can cause PTSD are: rape, car crashes, shootings in high schools, shootings in Orlando, like the after concert meet and greet where Christina Grimmie was murdered, seeing a vicious assault or finding a dead body in a dumpster, like one of my friends did when she was sixteen.

There are many events that can cause post-traumatic stress. Symptoms can include: nightmares, flashbacks, severe anxiety, and uncontrollable thoughts about the event. These symptoms can cause havoc on your nervous system, and your life, and cause you to become hyper-vigilante, interfering with your flight or fight response. They can make daily life very difficult for a while. You may have trouble coping, or adjusting, to a sense of normalcy after experiencing a traumatic event.

Sometimes the symptoms will gradually go away over time. Sometimes they may worsen, depending on the severity of the event, and your personal history. People with high levels of empathy can find recovering from PTSD tricky, as they feel things more keenly than the average person. If this is the case, it is important to find a good trauma expert to work with because there is a big difference between mental illness and trauma.

Post-traumatic stress is a normal reaction to an abnormal situation. There is nothing you did to cause the "*dis-order*" – it is caused by something that was done to you. With mental illness, there can be many factors depending on the condition, like depression, schizophrenia, borderline personality, and bi-polar. While people with PTSD may experience situational depression, it is not the same as being born with a genetic predisposition to depression.

The symptoms from PTSD can be scary, because each time you have a flashback or a repressed memory surfaces, it affects you on a physical level as if you were experiencing the event again and again. Your body cannot tell the difference between something that is happening right now, or something that you vividly imagine. The intrusive thoughts and flashbacks can feel as if you are re-experiencing the event repeatedly, and will produce the same physical sensations of shock, horror, and adrenaline that your body produced when the primary traumatic event occurred.

With many war veterans coming back into the country, we are learning more about trauma. More veterans commit suicide because of PTSD than are killed in battle. Having PTSD is a hellish experience.

What is complex post-traumatic stress?

Complex Post Traumatic Stress Disorder (C-PTSD) is a condition that results from chronic or long-term exposure to emotional trauma, over which a victim has little or no control, and from which there is little or no hope of escape, like in cases of domestic, emotional, physical or sexual abuse.

To heal from complex PTSD is not an overnight fix, you cannot "think" your way out of it. Having panic attack upon panic attack, day after day, night after night, messes up:

1. Your central nervous system
2. Your limbic system
3. Your endocrine system

I know, because I was diagnosed with it in 2015. It can make you feel like you are living in hell.

Since your mind does not know the difference between things you vividly imagine and events that are taking place, each time you have a flashback, or a repressed memory comes back, your body produces the same physical symptoms as it did when the trauma was taking place.

Your reactions escalate, and your body is filled with cortisol. People with complex post-traumatic stress often are hypervigilant throughout the day and night, without even knowing. This causes the muscles to be tense constantly, and never enter a state of relaxation. The tense muscles produced by hypervigilance is known as "body armor".

Your body produces so much cortisol when you are in levels of high stress repeatedly that you have the same reactions physically, as if you had been taking steroids for years.

Effects of too much stress on the body include:

1. Losing hair
2. Having tendon ruptures
3. Hearts attacks and high risk of heart attacks
4. Enlarged heart
5. Significant risk of liver disease
6. Liver cancer
7. Compromised immune system
8. Getting sick
9. Inflammation
10. Insomnia
11. Adrenal fatigue
12. Comprised nervous system and limbic system

I experienced many of the above symptoms full stop. At one point my CRP levels were over three hundred and fifty. CRP is C-Reactive Protein. Normal is three or under. High CRP levels indicate that there is inflammation in the heart, and that you may be at risk for a heart attack or stroke.

War veterans are at risk for Complex PTSD, as well as people who have been in abusive situations repeatedly. People who have been in cults, lived with sociopaths or targeted by emotional predators are also at risk. Women from abusive relationships or who have been in domestic violence situations can develop complex post-traumatic stress.

Having Complex PTSD is extremely overwhelming and can make your life feel unbearable. Friends and family may not understand, as they have no frame of reference for it. You may feel alienated and dismissed. Sometimes doctors will treat you dismissively, as the medical field is just learning of its effects and how to treat it.

People may turn to drugs or alcohol when they have untreated PTSD. This is completely understandable. Left untreated, Complex PTSD wreaks havoc on your life. I came to the point where I had a full breakdown and was unable to work for eighteen months. Once you get diagnosed with Post Traumatic Stress Disorder it is important to find a good trauma expert.

You must learn how to calm the nervous system and activate the parasympathetic system.

Things that activate the parasympathetic nervous system and stimulate the vagus nerve are essential, as well things that produce oxytocin levels in your body. Your body cannot produce oxytocin and cortisol levels at the same time. Think of it as Pac-Man. When your body produces oxytocin, it gobbles up the extra cortisol. Oxytocin can be purchased as a nasal spray which you take three times a day. Call on Archangel Raphael for help in healing your body and mind.

Ask the angels to lead you to the perfect experts who can best assist you in your healing process. Before you go to sleep at night time, imagine that a circle of loving angels are surrounding your bed. They are holding their hands toward you, instructing your limbic system and central nervous system to normalize. The angels are helping your amygdala and frontal cortex to work in a healthy manner. Imagine the angels filling your cells with healthy vibrant divine white light.

Angel Work Out

Please, if you suffer from flash backs, anxiety, panic attacks, seek help today. Do not wait. If you have a friend who has PTSD or Complex PTSD, be supportive, encouraging, and listen. Do not under any circumstances be dismissive of your friend's feelings or fears. People with PTSD have a hard time asking for help. You cannot "fix them", or be their therapist. But a kind word, and encouraging hug, can go a long way in a world of someone who has been affected by trauma.

Be especially supportive of them seeking help. You could save their life.

May the angels love, support, and surround you today and may you be led to the people, places, and experts who can best help you. May all beings be free from suffering. PTSD is treatable and curable. You can heal, but it will take time it is not something you can "think" your way out of. That is why it is important to find a trauma expert you feel safe with. The angels lead me to Sandy, the woman who helped me with my trauma. Sandy had a medical background and was the perfect match to help me. Ask the angels to lead you to the best help possible.

DAY FOURTEEN. THE ANGELS AND THE LAW OF ATTRACTION

What is the Law of Attraction?

There are many universal laws that work whether we are conscious of them or not. These laws have been around before mankind existed. There is the law of attraction, the law of grace, the law of karma and other universal laws.

The law of attraction was made mainstream by the book The Secret. I taught a Law of Attraction class for six years once a month and most of the people who came did so because they had read The Secret by Rhonda Bryne. They wanted to learn how to attract things they could be, do or have.

The law of attraction simply means like attracts like. When you use it with the help of the angels it gives the law of attraction a turbo boost. I have seen miracles happen not only in my life but in my clients, lives. On an hourly basis as well as a daily basis. This is not an exaggeration.

One client manifested a MacBook, she thought it would take six months, it happened in six days. Another client manifested fourteen thousand dollars within two months, one manifested seven hundred. I was doing a phone session with her and I kept getting for her to ask for about twenty thousand dollars but I knew on an intuitive level this would be too much for her. Women especially have a hard time receiving and are much better at giving.

I suggested to my client she ask for ten thousand dollars. Within five days she called me crying tears of happiness "Catherine I got seventeen thousand dollars, thank you so much" I replied I did nothing except pray for you and the angels used me to deliver messages for you so I am happy you got what you deserved but *you* did the work.

Whenever I had a session with someone I would start out asking that the people who could best benefit from my services find me and secondly that they will felt more uplifted and empowered after a session than before speaking with me. Sales people would often try to get me to buy advertising from them. I don't. Why? Because the law of attraction and the angels are so much better and faster and creative at bringing me what I need to do my work than any paid advertising. Sometimes the angels would suggest the best places for me to advertise so that is when I would pay for it.

How does the law of attraction work?

The law of attraction works like magnets. When you put two magnets together depending on which end you hold they either stick like glue to each other or will not touch at all. You can feel the energy repelling when you hold magnets together the "wrong" way.

All our brainwaves and emotions contain magnetic energy that we radiate out into the world.

When you are angry your emotional body radiates waves of anger energy. When you are sad, you radiate waves of sadness, when you think about things repeatedly you send those brainwaves or thought waves out into the world. These energetic waves can be measured. Brain waves are measured by counts per second.

There are five brain wave states:

Beta
Alpha
Delta
Theta
Gamma

Beta waves radiate at fourteen to forty counts per second (cps). This is the conscious waking state that we use for analytical thinking, reasoning and logic. Most of us are in the Beta state all of the day.

Alpha waves radiate at seven to fourteen cps. This is the state of deep relaxation, the state you are in when extremely relaxed. You can enter this state through yoga or meditation or by listening to alpha wave music. YouTube has a lot of alpha music.

Alpha is the most important state for doing angel work, creative work and for manifesting. This is also where your intuition is the strongest. If you want to get good at manifesting and using the law of attraction practice listening to alpha music for an hour a day. You can use it to study with or simply put some on while you do the housework or while you are doing work on your computer. I drop the volume down low while using alpha music when I write. The voice of Alpha is the voice of your intuition especially in the lower range under ten cps. To get good at psychic work and angel communication you must learn how to put your brain consciously into the alpha state. The quickest most effective way I know of to do this is listen to alpha music. If you listen to alpha music for fifteen minutes three times a day it will change your life.

Many people say they can't meditate. If you are one of these people start listening to alpha music with your eyes closed while sitting or lying down when you wake up, after lunch and before bedtime. Within three weeks you will notice a huge difference physically, mentally and emotionally, as well as sharpening your intuition.

I used to use alpha music three times a day everyday but after a while got busy and stopped doing it regularly.When I broke my ankle and the cast was removed I was in extreme pain. I hate painkillers. They increase anxiety and mess with your nervous system as well as having other horrid side effects. For my ankle to heal I had to start exercising it. The pain was intolerable. I committed to listening to alpha music three times a day. While listening, I would imagine my body healthy and strong. I would say "pain be gone," "ankle heal" "nervous system calm down" and other healing statements. Within three weeks I was walking unaided. It did take longer to strengthen my muscles.

You can use this technique for manifesting too. Daydream of things you would like to have be or do while listening to alpha music. This is the quickest technique I have found to manifest.

Theta waves are between four to seven cps. This is the sleep state or very deep meditation state. Theta waves are where you have lucid dreams or enter REM.

Delta waves are zero to four cps. This is the deep sleep wave. Your body needs time in delta for healing and replenishing. It needs time in theta for REM sleep. Sleep deprivation is a form of torture in some countries. When you don't sleep not only is your body physically exhausted but you will start to hallucinate if you go for a few days without sleep as your body tries to produce the REM state while you are awake.

Gamma brain waves radiate at over forty cps. Initial research shows gamma waves are associated with high level information processing and bursts of insight. I think people who have ADD or quick firing brains operate at Gamma frequently throughout the day. If this sounds like you, you must balance out your neural pathways by listening to alpha music for an hour a day.

It is just as important to take care of our mental health, emotional health, spiritual and psychic health as it is to take care of our physical health.

The law of attraction works best when you slow your brain waves down to alpha.

How to magnetize yourself to manifest things quickly

Listen to a piece of music that you love. Emotions have velocity, which is why if you change your emotional state quickly your mind will follow. Everything begins in the imagination but if you are using affirmations like "I know have two thousand dollars" but don't really believe it you are wasting your time.

Instead get yourself into a positive emotional state. There are several techniques you can use:

1. Listen to a piece of music you love
2. Watch a funny YouTube video
3. Write a list of three things you would like to attract.

Another angel miracle, my cd player in my car had not worked for nearly three years. I did not want to purchase a new cd player because it wasn't worth the money for the age of my car. I kept asking the angels to fix my CD player. On Monday February 7th 2010 one CD popped out. My son Logan was driving at the time. He said "mom put in a clean CD and see if it works. I had the master teachings of Abraham still in my car which I had not listened to for two years. I grabbed the first CD randomly. Immediately Abraham started talking about psychics! The law of attraction and angels work together in perfect synchronicity.

Angel Workout

List three things you would like to attract

Ask the angels to help you manifest them. Say; "Dear angels please lead me to the perfect opportunities that will help me manifest _____. Guide me as to what actions to take or where I should go. Give me the information that will best help me at this time."

"Please tell me one thing I can do today to begin the process of attracting my hearts desires, for the highest good of all. And so it is. Amen"

The law of attraction works like a magnet so to get the fastest results instead of saying affirmations change your emotions. Your emotions fuel your dreams, combine this with listening to alpha music for fifteen minutes once a day and asking the angels to help is a triple whammy. Things will start to manifest almost immediately. Especially when you do your part and act on the intuitive messages you are getting.

We are in constant co-creation with the universe. Using your mind and emotions thoughtfully will fast track you to the life you want to live. Action is often the step left out when learning about the law of attraction. It is a crucial part of manifesting. You ask, you listen to intuitive messages, you follow, you receive, you give thanks. What I have found is the angels will lead you to the next step like a parent holding a child's hand and guiding them in the right direction. It is one step at a time, then the angels give you the next step. The angels say "If we gave you humans too much information all at once, it would overwhelm you and you would be less likely to carry it out. Plus, you humans tend to forget things. When we spoon feed you step by step actions to take you seem to follow these instructions better.

What would you like to attract into your life today? Think about big things and little things. Start with something small, then practice asking for something big. The better you get at manifesting the more you will trust the process.

Angel Workout

Create a vision board using pictures from magazines or draw on paper things you would like to have, be or do. Spend about an hour doing this. Hang the picture where you will see it daily. Each day spend fifteen minutes' day dreaming about what it will feel like to have those items or qualities.

DAY FIFTEEN. THE ANGELS AND TELEPATHY

Understanding telepathy

Telepathy is the communication between people or spirit beings of thoughts, feelings and desires in ways that cannot yet be understood by scientific laws. Telepathy is sometimes also called thought transference. Thoughts are energy. They vibrate at a higher frequency than radio waves, and therefore cannot be measured the same way that radio waves can be measured. Feelings are energy, too. You can measure the effect feelings have on your body by taking your pulse rate when you are angry, depressed or happy, and noting the difference.

There are two types of conversation. These are verbal and non-verbal. When you talk out loud, you are communicating verbally. When you communicate without words, you are talking non-verbally. Telepathy is a form of non-verbal communication. Think about the last time you had a conversation with a friend. There were two levels to the conversation. One is the message you are conveying with your words. The second level is the messages you are conveying without words. This is non-verbal communication, and can be expressed through body language, posture, tone of voice, facial expression, actions and your eyes.

Think about the last time you were talking with your friend. Did her or his language, tone of voice, facial expression and actions match their words? If you replay the situation in your mind now, and turn off the volume as if you are watching a silent movie, what do you notice? Have you ever had the experience of listening to someone talk and known that what they were saying was not true? How did you know this? Most likely it was because you were picking up information from them that was non-verbal. Your impression of their actions and body language did not match the verbal message they were giving you.

Everybody can communicate non-verbally. You don't need to learn any special skills to begin. You simply need to become more aware of the nonverbal levels of communication that takes place around you. Each time you have a conversation with someone today begin to observe what is being communicated nonverbally. What kind of feelings do you pick up? You can learn to sense energy in others, and know what they are feeling, or thinking.

Your mind is like a satellite constantly picking up and sending out signals. Your mind thinks in images and pictures, more often than in words. You may get an impression of something in your mind. Throughout the day you receive many impressions in your mind in the form of pictures, or a sense about something. Wherever you go, to school, on the bus, the grocery store - your mind is constantly picking up thought forms and impressions from everything you see and hear. You can learn how to tune into the thought forms and impressions that you do want to receive, and how to tune out the thought forms and impressions you don't want to receive.

When I was a teenager, my best friend and I used to say we would send each other thought waves when we were apart from each other. We would send thought waves of love and good will to each other, and to certain boys we liked. We didn't know it at the time, but what we were doing was practicing telepathy. Telepathy is easy to learn and easy to practice. You already communicate non-verbally without realizing it. Now you can begin to communicate non-verbally consciously.

Whenever you have a thought about someone, you are sending a telepathic message. Thought waves are like radio signals – they go out into the atmosphere. Your thoughts are magnetic. There are three main ways of sending out telepathic thoughts:

1. Through your mind and imagination
2. Through your feelings
3. Through your eyes

You are always radiating what you are thinking about. Think about this. Let's say you are at work. Someone comes into the room, and you know instantly that he or she is in a bad mood, even though they haven't said anything. How do you know this? Because they are communicating through their actions, their facial expression and their eyes and posture.

The two main ways of communicating telepathically are through mental telepathy and emotional telepathy.

Mental telepathy

With mental telepathy, you receive impressions in the form of pictures, images, words or feelings directly into your mind or imagination. Sometimes you may get a sense of something in your mind, rather than seeing an exact image. You may hear an inner voice, or see an inner picture, and feel an inner knowing. You receive thought waves in your mind, and you can send them from your mind too. Your third eye or brow chakra is located between your eyebrows. This is the energy center that enables you to receive and send mental messages.

How to send mental messages

If you want to send a mental message to someone, simply hold a thought in your mind. Ask the person's divine self for permission to send a message. If it feels comfortable, send them a message of love, light or good will.

Do not consciously send people angry or vengeful messages. Whatever you send out will come back to you.

How to receive mental messages

There are three main ways of receiving non-verbal messages:

1. Through your mind or third eye chakra

This is the best way to receive telepathic messages, because you don't have to take on the other person's energy in your body to understand what they are thinking or feeling. You can observe the energy, or receive mental messages very clearly, without it changing your own energy or moods.

2. Through your feelings

These are the non-verbal thoughts you receive in your emotional body. Very often you feel things in your emotional body through your physical body. Let's say you are in a situation where you suddenly feel afraid. How do you know you are afraid? You might get a panicky feeling in your stomach. If someone is angry with you, you might feel his or her anger in the pit of your stomach.

The non-verbal thoughts you receive through your emotional body are transmitted to you via your solar plexus chakra. Your solar plexus chakra is located just under your rib cage in the center of your body. When you receive telepathic messages, this way you are vulnerable to taking on other people's energy. You can tell if you have taken on their energy by how you feel after you have spent time with them. Maybe you are visiting with a friend who is very down about her life. She has just spent the last hour crying on your shoulder. You feel sorry for her, and of course want to help her. You spend time listening and sympathizing. When you leave her, you feel extremely tired and a bit down yourself, even though you felt good before you arrived. She feels cheered up, and now you feel exhausted. What has happened? You have taken her energy on through your emotional body.

You can learn to receive telepathic messages only through your mind. This is the most productive form of telepathy, because you will pick up others' feelings and thoughts without having to take on their energy too. When you receive impressions through your emotional body, you take on the other person's energy as well. To avoid this, simply imagine you have a beautiful spinning wheel of light circling around your solar plexus like a fan. Other people's energy cannot penetrate through this fan of light into your body.

3. Through your eyes

If someone sends you a 'dirty' look, you receive their energy through your eyes. If someone is totally in love with you, you can receive the energy of love from them through their looks of adoration. You can sense other's disapproval, like or dislike from the messages they send you with their eyes.

Angel workout

Practice noticing what kinds of messages people are sending you through their eyes. Then begin to practice receiving the messages in your mental body rather than in your emotional body. Make a conscious decision to do this. Begin to observe from your eyes, rather than pick up intuitive information in your feelings. Many of you are highly empathetic, and therefore more susceptible to picking up others' feelings. You can learn to receive impressions through your third eye by observing others without taking on their feelings.

How to block telepathic messages

If you think about someone and get an unpleasant feeing of any kind like irritation, hurt, anger or sadness, imagine light flooding through your mind. Call light to the situation by saying: "Divine light, radiate through me now. I ask you to bring your healing qualities to these feelings."

See the person and the surrounding feelings dissolving in your imagination. Do this as often as necessary.

If someone gives you a dirty look, you can block it by calling divine light to you and radiating as much light as you can muster. Your good feelings will cancel out the other person's ill wishes. You can also seal your aura by imagining you are in a clear human hamster ball.

Begin to talk to your guardian angel telepathically

When you are ready to talk to your guardian angel, send him or her a mental message. You imagine what you want to say. You may say "guardian angel help!" or "guardian angel be here now!" All you need to do is talk to your guardian angel in your imagination.

Opening to Telepathy

Read this exercise through a couple of times first before practicing it, so you know what to do.

There are three steps you need to follow to start developing the skills necessary to practice telepathy. These are:

1. Relax your body
2. Clear your mind
3. Open to receive messages

Relax your body

The best time to practice telepathy is just before bedtime or at a time when the house is quiet. Lock yourself in your bedroom, and get away from distracting noises like a blaring television set or rowdy stereo. You might like to take a warm bath and soak for twenty minutes to relax all your muscles.

Make sure it has been a couple of hours since you have last eaten. A heavy stomach full of food can dull your psychic facilities. If you are hungry have a light snack.

Put some relaxing music. You can choose music that has been specially written for getting in touch with your angels, or classical music from the baroque era. Music that is set in nature, or music with Tibetan bells, is a great choice, also.

Lie on your bed. Make sure you are comfortably warm. You might like to put a blanket over you. Consciously relax your muscles starting with your toes, ask your toes to relax and move up each body part asking them in turn to relax – your knees, your legs, your torso, your arms, your neck and shoulders, then finally your head.

Clear your mind

Imagine you are floating on a beautiful white soft cloud. This cloud is as big as a football field. You feel so comfortable and cozy, floating on this beautiful big cloud.

Now imagine that your body and mind is being flooded with light, like the floodlights at a football field. You feel this beautiful white light pouring in through the top of your head washing away any doubts, worries, fears or concerns from the day. You feel your mind expand with this brilliant white light. The light flows down through the rest of your body. You feel your energy sparkle with the vibrancy of this dancing white light.

Open to receive messages

You now feel totally relaxed. You consciously direct your mind to begin receiving mental messages from your guardian angel by saying: "I open my mind to receive spiritual imprints from my guardian angel. I instruct my mind to open to receiving pictures, thoughts, words or sensations from my guardian angel. I know I am divinely protected and I ask my guardian angel to ensure I only receive messages from him or her."

Imagine that you have a third eye in your forehead between your brows. This third eye is open and can see energy clearly.

How to receive mental messages from your guardian angel

Now you are ready to begin receiving telepathic messages from your guardian angel. In your imagination see a picture of your guardian angel. Imagine your angel as beautiful and radiant as possible. Don't worry if you can't clearly see your angel in your imagination. Get a sense of your angel.

Ask your guardian angel a question in your mind.

Allow the answer to form in your imagination either as a picture, an image or as words. Sometimes, you will see a mental movie playing out in your imagination. Sometimes, you may get a sense of the answer or feel it in your mind. Other times, you may hear an inner voice that speaks in complete sentences, or you may simply receive two or three words. Don't strain, simply allow the answer to surface easily and effortlessly.

Angel Workout

Practice sending thought waves to someone you love tonight. Imagine the person sitting in front of you. Have a conversation with them as if they are in the room. During the next day see if you get any signs that remind you of this person. For further practice go to my YouTube channel and watch the videos on telepathy.

DAY SIXTEEN. HOW TO DO AN ANGEL READING

Doing an angel reading can be fun and insightful. Any form of divination is a way of foretelling the future based on what is happening now. We each have about three to four probable futures. Even if you believe in destiny, your destiny can change. Nothing is written in stone. Not even the time you will die.

I believe we each have several exit points where we can leave the planet. For example, I could have died when I had periodontitis, and I saw the angels and my dad on the bridge of light. I chose to stay. But I don't think I will live much longer than seventy-four. When we are married or in a serious relationship; our destinies are intertwined with our partner. Once the relationship ends, our destinies are no longer together.

Destiny is different from fate. Destiny is the events that will happen to a person or situation in the future. Fate is the hidden power believed to control future events. I don't believe in fate as defined above. I do believe there are patterns and cycles in the universe, in our solar system and galaxies, within our bodies, and in the cycles of the seasons and the tides. I believe some things are destined to happen and sometimes Life Happens.

For example, I believe it is impossible NOT to meet your soulmates. At some time your paths are bound to cross if you listen to your intuition, but that doesn't mean it might be a love interest or a relationship without challenges. All relationships have challenges. Even Buddha said relationships were one of the most difficult territory to navigate through on the earth place. Which is why a lot of spiritual leaders, monks or nuns practice celibacy.

Doing a reading when foretelling events in the future; is based upon what is going on in your life now. When it comes to timelines, unless you are speaking in generalities, it is harder to read. When you do a reading generally what shows up is what will happen in the next three months depending on your actions. The longer the timeline for questions asked the thinner the etheric cords into the future.

To do a card reading;

What supplies you need:

- ♥ A pack of tarot cards
- ♥ A pack of angel oracle cards
- ♥ Some meditation music
- ♥ A quiet room where you won't be interrupted

A pack of tarot cards is useful because they give you a more in-depth reading than just using oracle cards. There are many beautiful decks on the market, including angel tarot cards. I recommend using the Universal Rider Waite deck as a beginning deck. The imagery of the tarot is a pictorial language. So even if you don't know all the cards meanings, or don't want to learn tarot, that's fine. Having a deck will give you a deeper reading. You are reading the cards like you would read a painting. You don't have to know the original meanings, just as you don't have to know why the artist painted the subject matter the way he did. What matters most is what you see in the card. How you interpret it, just as if you were "reading" a painting in an art gallery.

You need a quiet room because you need a place where it will be easy for you to tune in to what the angels want to tell you. Your bedroom or even the bathroom will do.

To choose cards, just go to your local bookstore or look on Amazon and choose a deck that has pictures you like. What I recommend is looking at different decks on Amazon, if you don't have a store nearby with sample decks. Do a Google search for the deck you like. Click on images and see if the pictures appeal to you. Then buy the deck.

Can you do a reading without cards?

Absolutely, you can channel angel info instead. We will talk a bit about both ways today. If you decide to channel a reading, you will need a voice recorder on your phone or computer. And a quiet space with some meditation music to do your reading in. You can look for meditation music on Pandora, Spotify, YouTube, iTunes, or your favorite music place. The reason we use music during a reading is because it provides an easy way for your brain to get into an alpha state, which makes you more receptive to angel messages.

A reading with cards

To start, turn on the music, close the door of the room you are in, and get comfortable. Start with a prayer: "Dear angels, may the information that best helps me come through in a clear and specific manner for the highest good of all, May I be a channel for divine love and divine guidance. Archangel Gabriel, be here with me now, And so it is. Amen." You can also ask your guardian angel, your spirit guide or any other angel to be with you too.

Think of five questions you want to ask. Make a list of these questions. Make them open-ended questions, not yes/no questions. Shuffle the cards while you think of your questions. For each question, pull a tarot card and an angel oracle card. Read the meaning of the card both literally from the booklet provided in the deck, and by gazing at the card and meditating on it, until you connect with it emotionally. What does the card say to you? What is the picture saying? What is the emotions you are picking up from the card? Don't worry if you think you are doing it right, or wrong. Just do it anyway. You will get better with practice.

Make a note of the answers you got to each question in your angel journal. In a month's time, read the questions and answers, and note how much happened the way you 'saw' it in the cards. If you know how to do a Celtic cross reading, then do that if you'd like. But for the purposes of this book, we are keeping it simple. Either way, the information will help you.

A reading without cards

In many ways, doing a reading without cards is easier. You don't have to have a deck of cards. You can connect directly to the angels without shuffling and dealing. Some of my clientele prefer card readings, and some prefer mediumship, or channeling. To do a reading without cards, use the same prayer as above: "Dear angels, may the information that will best help me come through in a clear and specific manner for my highest good."

Have a list of five questions on a piece of paper. Play some meditation or alpha wave music in the background if you like. Close your eyes and count backwards from fifty to one. This calms your mind making it more receptive to angel guidance. Turn on your voice recorder, open your eyes and read aloud question one. Close your eyes and say: "Dear angel, please speak through me to answer my question." Then begin speaking whatever comes into your mind. Don't edit, don't censor, don't even think. You are using your creative mind to tune into divine source. Just answer the question with whatever words pop into your mind.

Repeat this process with your next four questions. Then thank the angels: "Dear angels, thank you for giving me the information that will best help me today." Turn off your voice recorder. Wait a day or two, and then play back your reading. Make a note in your calendar to listen to the recording again in a month from today. In your angel journal write down any thoughts, impressions, things that happened, and note how accurate the information was. Remember this is supposed to be fun and light. You are not studying for a PhD in angel communication!

A reading for a friend.

If you would like to practice doing a reading for a friend, use either of the above methods.

Firstly, sit at a table with your friend across from you. Take hold of his or her hands, close your eyes, and ask your friend to close their eyes too. Pray: "Dear angels, may the information that will best help _____(their name) come through in a clear and specific manner. May I be a conduit for divine guidance and divine light. Archangel Gabriel, help me communicate clearly and may both our guardian angels be present to help too.

You can do a reading using cards, or using the channeling method. If you use the channeling method, ask your friend to turn their voice recorder on. Even the free Google docs voice recorder is a good method, because then you have a written record.

Trust your intuition. Trust that the angels are on your side. Trust that you can do this. And trust that the more you practice, the better you will get at it. If you decide to charge for your readings one day, ask the angels what to charge. And remember, we all have bills to pay. Just as you wouldn't expect your accountant or mechanic to work for you for free, neither should you work for free.

Angel Workout

Of course, you know I am going to say practice doing an angel reading on yourself. Go on. You can do it. Ask the angels to help you.

DAY SEVENTEEN. TIPS FOR PROFESSIONAL READERS

Doing readings for other people is both fun and rewarding, but it can also be very challenging and draining at times. You need to get clear in your head, and on paper, what your own guidelines for readings are. Unlike therapists, psychic readers or angel readers don't get trained in how to set limits and boundaries with clients, where to draw the line between friendship and clients, or how much money to charge.

If you are reading professionally, you must always be ethical and honest. There are unfortunately too many scam artists out there, like any profession, who give the psychic or angel readings a bad name. One horror story I heard recently was from a woman who had called a psychic in Texas, who claimed she could reunite lovers within twenty-four hours. The psychic charged four hundred and fifty dollars prepaid via a credit card online, with a number to call once you had paid. This woman who had paid the four hundred and fifty dollars never got her reading, because the so-called psychic's phone box had a message that said her message box was full, and could not accept any messages. The woman never got her reading, and when she called me, was understandably distressed.

One of my friends paid a psychic seven thousand dollars to bring back his girlfriend. Never pay anyone to reunite you with an ex. My friend spent seven thousand dollars and his girlfriend did not return. He did find a new one. Please don't answer the 'reunite lovers' advertisements. I disabled comments on my YouTube channel due to all the 'psychics' who were leaving spam to reunite lovers on my channel. No one can promise you they will reunite you with an ex-partner. This is called exploitation not psychic healing.

To maintain ethical standards within the psychic professionally community, we must set our own guidelines.

These are some of mine:

Never say you can do something when you can't. For example, I don't locate missing items or lost people. I have a basic knowledge of astrology, but am by no means an astrologer.

I prefer to say "I do psychic readings" or "I do angel readings" rather than "I'm a psychic". There's nothing wrong with saying you are a psychic, just say what feels right to you.

Never claim you are a hundred per cent accurate. I tell clients a good psychic is about 80 percent accurate, this is because we have different probable futures. What a good reading will do is provide insight and clarity into the current situation, and what a couple of the probable outcomes could be. However, there are exceptions to this rule. I would never claim to be a hundred percent accurate. I just don't think this is true. The type of readings I used to give were spiritual counseling, and teaching clients skills and tools on how to empower themselves, rather than become dependent on me.

I use tarot in two ways: one as a pictorial language, and secondly as a prompt for my clairvoyance. I find the richness of symbolism in tarot cards much more in depth than some of the angel decks available. That said, Pamela Mathews has created a wonderful deck called the Aura Soma tarot that is rich in both tarot symbolism, and angels and ascended masters. I highly recommend it. You can get it from Pamela's website www.grail.co.nz. Pamela also has a deck called the seventy-two angels of the kabbalah. These decks are designed to work together and create the most in-depth card reading system I have used.

When you are reading the cards, they usually prompt clairvoyance. Starting and finishing with an angel prayer "frames" the reading.

Delivering angel messages is a joy and a pleasure. I find they work extremely well with tarot cards, and the angels can give you specifics that get prompted by certain cards. I also get flashes of insight, like I did this morning when doing a reading, and I correctly named the school a client was attending. I also always pray that the money my clients pay me is blessed and multiplied ten times back to them.

Decide a price range that is right for you. When I first started doing psychic readings, I asked the angels what a fair price was, and they said twenty dollars for fifteen minutes and a dollar per minute after that. A couple of years later, I changed my rates to sixty dollars for 30 minutes an hour.

Decide if you want to be pre-paid for phone readings. I used to let people pay afterwards, and sometimes with old clients I still do. However, I got burned a few times by people not paying, or paying months later. For face-to-face readings, clients can pay after their session.

Decide what kind of clientele you want. When you are reading at a metaphysical bookstore, you take the clients that show up. However, when I got my own office I could choose what kind of clients I wanted to take. This goes back to your areas of expertise, for example, like I said, I don't locate missing items, but I love doing romance readings, relationship readings, past lives, auras, life purpose and angel readings. I love channeling messages from the angels, and I love teaching people how to connect to their own angels too.

Always keep a suicide crisis phone line handy. Sometimes clients may need professional medical help, or simply a safe place to vent their feelings. There are free national services that offer this kind of support, so keep those numbers handy to refer to if necessary.

Do not let clients abuse you

Some clients can be unintentionally abusive. Until I learned to set strong boundaries, some clients (and friends) were acting as if I was a twenty-four-hour psychic hotline, or would bring gifts and expect a free reading.

They would also give me all kinds of things to do that did not fall under my services, like wanting me to read manuscripts they had written, or to "drop in" for a visit, and end up asking questions; essentially, I was doing a free reading. Keep a strong boundary between clients and friends. Just as you wouldn't go out for lunch with your therapist, don't go out for lunch with a client. Socializing with clients is not good business practice. When friends come for a reading keep your professional hat on and charge them. While doing a reading professionally keep your standards the same for friends and clients. When a friend asks for a reading outside your hours simply say, "I'm not working right now, let me book you in for a session tomorrow if you want a reading."

Stick to the time scheduled

This is important both for you and your client. I start walking people to the door when their time is up, or if I am on the phone, I gently say, let's wrap up with a prayer.

How to handle difficult clients

Ninety-nine per cent of the time clients are wonderful. But occasionally you may run into clients who are skeptical, or even a little aggressive. I try to make the client feel as comfortable as possible if I feel the session isn't going well, or there is tension in the air. I gently ask if there is something wrong. Occasionally I have said: "I want you to get the best value for your money, and I'm not sure I'm the best reader for you. I have a list of other readers I can refer you to if you would like."

Schedule breaks for yourself

This is extremely important. Wash your hands between each session. This simple act washes off the energy between each reading. Have a quick shower when you get home to wash off the psychic imprints you have picked up throughout the day. Take a three-day weekend once a month. Avoid burnout. I took two months off once, because I was so burned out. That's when I decided to get clearer in my head about what my guidelines for readings were. Always invoke a circle of angelic protection around the reading and ask the angels to give you the information that will best help your client today. Take a two-week break when you can afford it. Over summer, I tended to do more phone readings, as I wanted to spend more time with my children.

Doing readings takes a lot of energy. Most people don't realize how draining it can be, so it's crucial that you protect, nourish and replenish yourself and your office space. You may find yourself changing work times as your lifestyle changes. Currently, I write fulltime and work between 9am and 5pm with a two-hour lunch break Monday through Friday. My sons are adults and some of my friends have children. I take Thursday mornings off to spend time with friends. Making time for yourself is not selfish it is essential.

How to market yourself

The best marketing practices I have found is a business card with your photo on it. People can relate to photos, and it gives a personal touch to your card. When you finish a reading, give two cards to your clients. Say: "Here is one for you, and here is one for a friend you think might enjoy a reading, or just leave it someplace."

I sprinkled my business cards wherever I would go. They are more effective than flyers. People can pick them up and put them in their pockets. I would leave them at carwashes, bookstores, cafes, and toilets in restaurants. You never know who may stumble across one. This was one of my most effective forms of advertising.

A website is crucial. If you put your website address on your business cards, you will allow people to look up what you do. Decide what you want your website to be about. If it is specifically designed to get people to book a reading from you, make it as easy as possible for them to do that.

The final thing that I found beneficial is using a sandwich board sign that you can place outside your office, that says psychic readings are available here now. It's great for drive-by traffic, and lets people know that you are in your office. I would put mine out each day that I was at my office, and bring it in when I go home.

But the most important thing of course is to pray that the clients who can most benefit from your services will find you. Believe me, they will start showing up.

Angel Workout

Have you had a professional reading?

If you are a life coach or spiritual counselor, what ways do you replenish yourself?

What areas of your practice would you like to ask the angels for help with?

DAY EIGHTEEN. THE ANGELIC COUNCIL OF LIGHT

Where Do Angels Live?

Angels live all around us. They exist on the earth plane as enlightened beings, or bright shining lights, and intercede between heaven and earth continually throughout the day.

Many cultures believe there are different levels of consciousness, and different planes of existence. Most ancient cultures taught there were four levels of consciousness, and four planes of existence. In the Shamanic tradition, there is the upper world, the middle world and the lower world. A lot of indigenous people come from Shamanic traditions. The ancient Celtic civilization believed in the three worlds, just as the Māori from New Zealand do, and the Aztec and Toltec traditions from South America. In the shamanic world-view, the upper world is where angels live, and where star beings and other celestial realms are. The middle world is our realm, the earthly realm, but within this realm there are many realms, as too with the lower realm where our ancestors and spirit guides are said to dwell. The realm of spirit that is all around us is the fourth plane.

We live in patterns because we must. The Universe/multiverse is a pattern. So are we. Our bodies are a maze of patterns with each of us having unique fingerprints, and unique spiritual DNA. We live between two states of existence, the spiritual, and the mundane. And the macrocosm of the entire universe seems to be contained within each human in a similar pattern.

Most traditions say there are four levels of consciousness

1. The physical
2. The emotional
3. The mental
4. The spiritual

The physical represents our bodies, how we nourish them, exercise them, what we ingest, how we treat them. Some people take better care of their cars than they do their bodies. Then there is the emotional body. How do you take care of yourself on an emotional level? Some people have no emotional intelligence at all, and go around emotionally throwing up over everyone they encounter all day long.

You can choose to calm your emotions, and learn how to act in any given situation, rather than how to react as if you're on autopilot. Martial artists know the benefits of not acting from emotion. For example, if you are upset about something someone did, it is better to tell the person you are upset, and ask if you can talk about when you've had time to cool off or think things through, rather than reacting in the moment. This can lead to arguments or things being said that you will regret later.

The mental body is of course your mind, and you can choose where to put your mental focus. Meditation is a good practice for learning how to tame your mind. When you train your mind just as you train your body when you exercise, you develop mental acuity that will hold you in good stead throughout the day. Our minds are the doorway to the spiritual realm, because it is through the doorway of our imagination or during meditation or dream state that we access the spiritual realm. These planes exist within our own bodies as well as a template for the cosmos.

What is interesting is that if you study different cultures, you will find many cultures have four planes of existence and thirty-one levels of experience. In the western mystical tradition, there are four worlds and the ladder of light. Some people might refer to this as the stairway to heaven.

The four worlds are:

1. The physical world
2. The psychological world
3. The mental world
4. The spiritual world

The Ladder of Light

In the Bible, the ladder of light is referred to by Jacob as the fiery ladder of light that he saw angels ascending to heaven and descending to earth on, implying that this activity takes place on a regular basis.

The four worlds consist of:

1. The world of experience
2. The world of consciousness
3. The world of mind – the world of higher self
4. The world of insight

Within each of these four worlds are thirty-two stages of experience.

This belief stems from many traditions and cultures.

In the chakra system, there is the physical body, the emotional/astral body, the mental body and the spiritual body. Just as there are four different planes of existence within our bodies, there are four planes of existence in the spiritual realms too.

In the yoga system from India, there are seventy-two thousand nadis. Nadis is a term for the channels through which, in traditional Indian medicine, the energies of the physical body, the subtle body and the causal body are said to flow. Within this philosophical framework, the nadis are said to connect at special points of intensity called nadichakras. In basic chakra education, you learn there are seven chakras in your body. The crown, brow, throat, heart, solar plexus, belly and sacral chakras.

When studying chakra's in more depth you will learn there are seventy-two thousand chakras' in your body. These are the meridian points or nadis the yogic tradition refers to. These points are the same as the meridian points acupuncturists use.

Our bodies have thirty-six trillion cells. Each of these cells could be considered a mini chakra. In meditation, try imagining each of your thirty-six trillion cells spinning with divine white light, and imagine them healthy and balanced.

What is the Angel Council?

The Angel Council exists of the ten archangels, the seventy-two angels and other archangels and angels. Just as new humans and stars are born every minute, so too are new angels. We have more angels available to us now than at any other time on earth, the angels say. Call on them all day long for help and guidance, because the angels will show up whenever you ask. Over the next twelve days, you are going to learn about the ten archangel's I am referring to, and the seventy-two angels. But you can start visiting the angel realm now. You don't have to know the names of the angels to go there. Just ask the angels to take you there.

How can the angel council counsel you?

You can visit the Angel Council of Light in any of the four planes, or you can go to the Angel Palace. The key word for the angel palace is "completeness, paradise or perfection". You can reach the Angel Palace through your emotions, your imagination, your dreams or meditation. Ask the angels to take you for a visit to the angel palace. That's what I did. The gifts of the angel palace are perfection, divine happiness, and divine love. Everything comes full circle like the end of the hero's journey.

The Angel Council reminds us to live in the here and now, and it is this point of existence which is the most important. You can visit the Angel

Council at the Angel Palace to ask any questions. Think of it like a big round table where the ten archangels sit, and other angels come and go, including your guardian angel and your angel guide. This is where the angels come to get their training, and to carry out their tasks. They also get their to-do lists for helping humans who ask.

Whenever you are facing a major problem, ask the angels to take you to the Angel Palace so you can sit at the round table and consult with all ten archangels, or you can ask to consult one-on-one with any of the archangels or seventy-two angels, plus any other angels to get divine guidance on what your next move should be. For example, this morning I was having writer's block. I only had two chapters left to write, and then I was moving halfway across the world. I was feeling overwhelmed at what I had to accomplish. I asked the angels for their advice or counsel. They said: "Start at the most fun place in the chapter to write, then go from there". That helped with the writer's block. When I asked about moving, they said: "Don't freak out, haven't we always helped you before? Why would we stop now?"

"That's not helping," I replied. "You don't have to look for a place to live, get settled, set up a new home." "We have always led you to the best places to live, and we will this time too. Stop freaking out and just be here now. When the time comes to move, we will help you find a new place to live and get settled. Take baby steps, you don't have to do all this overnight." I am happy to report I moved back to California and the angels came through with their help.

My experience of the Angel Kingdom

I have visited the angel realm and other celestial realms in my dreams, in visions, in shamanic journeying, and during meditation or channeling sessions. Each time I have been, I am astounded at how beautiful it is. You can also use astral projection to visit each plane of existence, and to go to the Angel Kingdom. Remote viewing is another metaphysical skill that is good for visiting different planes.

One of the times I visited was just after my dad died. My dad and I had a running joke that he wasn't allowed to die until I had a book published. Dad would always laugh when I said this, and say; "I'll do my best Catherine!"

After my book, Teen Goddess was published, I went to visit my dad in Hawaii with my two young sons. I handed him a copy of the book that I had dedicated to him, and he died three days later.

About three weeks after his death, I had a dream where he came to show me what he was doing on the other side. It was the most beautiful place I have ever seen. There were gardens and statues everywhere, flowers, and lots of pools of water. Every building was dazzling white, and Dad showed me where he was "working" on the other side.

Another time, I had a dream where the angels took me to what they said in my dream was the Angel Palace. The buildings where sparkling white, and the colors more vivid than any I have seen on earth. The angels took me to an "angel nightclub" which was within the Angel Palace. The nightclub reminded me of something out of a Star Wars movie. Instead of drinking beer and dancing to loud music, there were relaxing couches everywhere. There were oxygen bars and soothing music. It was a lot of fun, and the angels seemed to communicate telepathically. I remember a feeling of joy and happiness, and that it was very peaceful and the colors were gorgeous. Everything was so clean. And there were big crystals and the nightclub was all white and peaceful, like a spa.

Angel workout for today

For the rest of the book you are going to learn about "Jacob's ladder" or the "ladder of light", the spheres that each Archangel rules, and which angels are under them.

You will learn about the Tree of Life. The Tree of Life, the ladder of light and the flower of life exist not only in Christian and Jewish mystical writings, but also in metaphysical writings, ancient texts and modern writings.

Some people refer to the Tree of Life as a static symbol. But one of the reasons the Tree of Life was named a tree was because it implies growth. A tree is not static. Each of the points on the tree (the spheres or planets) may be fixed (although they expand too, and move through time and space. Any act of creation can be represented by a tree. A tree and a flower are an act of creation. We began on a universal level as an act of creation, and each of us individually are acts of creation. In turn, we ourselves are meant to create.

Angel Workout

Today all I ask you to do is think about the many patterns and cycles in your own life.

Think about the patterns and cycles in the universe.

How are these similar?

What do you notice?

Do you notice any changes in your temperament that seem to be affected by the seasons? The phases of the moon? The time of the day?

When the ancient Romans named the planets, they named them after gods and goddesses. Not because they thought that the Gods lived up in the sky, or on these planets, but because they were describing the energy of the planet on an astrological and astronomy level.

If you went to the Angel Palace today, what would you like to ask your angel counselors?

DAY NINETEEN. THE HIERARCHY OF ANGELS

Angel experts like Thomas Aquinas, who have been writing about angels since the Middle Ages, believe there are nine choirs of angels. To me, this means there are nine races of angels. Just as there are different races of humans, dogs and cats and other sentient beings; angels can also be classified through certain races. I have started using the word family to describe them for simplicity's sake and the head of each as queen or king. This is purely to help you understand something complicated as easily as possible.

As I wrote earlier there are many different translations from when all these ideas were written and translated and many different variations. For example, each sephirot on the tree of life is a spinning wheel of light and carries different energy. Some traditions switch the sephiroth which Raphael and Michael rule, I am using the tradition I was taught.

There are nine groups (or choirs) of angels. The highest class of angels is known as the Angels of contemplation. These include the Seraphim at the top of the angel hierarchy; they are considered the most powerful, as they are the closest to divine source or God. Then there are Cherubim and the thrones. They are listed in order of power and authority.

The Angel Hierarchy:

The angels of contemplation who rule over all of creation

1. The Seraphim
2. The Cherubim
3. The Thrones

The angels who govern the universe (or multiverse)

4. The Dominions
5. The Powers
6. The Virtues

The angels who rule over the world. These are the angels closest to the earthly realm.

7. The Principalities
8. The Archangels
9. The Angels, including guardian angels

The middle group of angels receives its instructions from the angels of contemplation, and they in turn give instructions to the angels who rule over the world. Seraphim are considered so bright that for a human eye to see them, it could blind you. If you do see one; that's how dazzlingly bright and powerful a source of pure energy that they are.

You can see angels with your heart as well as with your physical eyes, and with clairvoyance. Each angel has a distinct personality and "job", or area of expertise. They work co-operatively as a race of beings for the greater good of all involved.

Angels are expressions of divine source, just as stars, oceans and flowers are. Angels are pure energy of love, joy, abundance, creativity, beauty, protection, and guidance. They are divine expressions of the great creator. And in the next chapter, you will meet the seventy-two angels of the year, each of who have a specific function, and rule for twenty minutes every day and four days a year.

Angels want to be actively involved in your life. They want to help you navigate through your problems and celebrate your successes. They want to help you achieve. They want to help you achieve your dreams, overcome difficulties you may be facing, navigate through tough times, protect you when you need it, comfort you when you are down and guide you to your greater good.

There are three important terms you should know about before we go further

1. The Tree of Life
2. The Ladder of Light
3. The Flower of Life

The Tree of Life

Each wheel on the tree of life is ruled by a different angel who you will meet on each day of the archangels. Each archangel rules eight angels from the seventy-two angels. Ancient mystics used a tree as a metaphor because it is a living growing organism, always expanding and contracting just as the universe we live in does.

The Ladder of Light

The Ladder of Light is sometimes called Jacob's Ladder. The ladder of light is the fiery ladder that Jacob saw the archangel Uriel ascend and descend on. This ladder can be used as a diagram to explain the different levels of ascension we go through, and as a map of creation. On a physical level, we each have a ladder of light within us. This is like Kundalini energy in the yogic tradition.

If you think of the angels as family's it makes it easier because technically Michael is not an Archangel. He is a seraph who rules The Powers. Saying Michael is the King of The Powers is easier than saying he is a seraphim. Each of the eight angels governed by their respective ruling angel have qualities that blend well with their commanding angel. For example; Chamuel rules from September 2 to October 4, the eight angels under her are Yehuiah, Lehahiah, Khaviah, Aniel, (not to be confused with Haniel), Haamiah, Reheal and Yeiazel.

Think of this system as angel astrology. March was the first month of the year in the ancient Roman Calendar. The Greeks and the Romans are responsible for naming our planets and for the system of western astrology we use today. Aries starts around March nineteenth depending on the moon since the astrological calendar is a lunar calendar not a solar calendar. The Roman calendar was reformed in 45 BC by Julius Caesar when it changed from a lunar calendar into a solar calendar. Previously calendars were lunisolar to align with the annual cycle of the sun and monthly cycle of the moon which takes 29.5 days.

The Gregorian Calendar which we follow in the western world was introduced in 1582 as a refinement of the Julian Calendar. The Gregorian Calendar is the default world calendar for secular purposes, although some countries follow their own calendar for celebrations and traditions but use the Gregorian as de-facto for business. This year Chinese New Year which is a lunisolar calendar was January 27th in the Southern Hemisphere and January 28th in the Northern. In Chinese astrology 2017 is the year of the rooster.

The Flower of Life

The Flower of Life is the modern name given to a geometrical figure composed of multiple evenly-spaced, overlapping circles, that are arranged so that they form a flower-like pattern with a six-fold symmetry like a hexagon. The Flower of Life holds a secret symbol created by drawing thirteen circles out of the *Flower of Life*. By doing this, you can discover the most important and sacred pattern in the universe. This is the source of all that exists; it's called the *Fruit of Life*. It contains thirteen informational systems. Each one explains another aspect of reality. These systems can give us access to everything ranging from the human body to the galaxies.

The complete flower contains the Kabbalah's Tree of Life, the fruit, the egg and the seed of life. The Tree of Life contains information about each of the archangels, and how they can help you. There are three triangles on the Tree of Life that represent a different level of existence, as well as Malkuth, The Kingdom, that represents earth and our bodies, especially the feet.

The definitions of each of the nine groups of angels and the triangles are:

The first triangle from the Tree of Life is: The world of emanations, this correlates to your spiritual being, divine self or higher self. The three archangels in this sphere are Metatron, Zafkiel and Raziel. They rule the crown chakra and the brow chakra or third eye.

Seraphim: The word seraph means fiery one. Seraphim are often described as having four-sided faces. The leader of the Seraphim is Metatron, who rules divine will. The Seraphs work on the spiritual level with elevated ideals, ascended thought and on opening communication with divine source through the crown chakra. They are associated with the planet Neptune. Each of the nine groups of angels is assigned to a different planet, except for Pluto.

My feelings on this is that angels as a race are growing, just as humans as a race are growing. They are not static, with a specific number who populate the earth. Angels continue to evolve and be born just as stars and planets do. The word Seraph comes from the root word meaning to shine, or burn brightly. Their light is so bright, that human beings would be immediately disintegrated if they looked at one.

Cherubim: A cherub is one of the angels who also attend directly to divine will. Most of us, when we think of cherubs, think of cute little baby angels with arrows on Valentine's Day. Cherubim are not little chubby cheeked baby angels. They are strong, tall, powerful angels.

Traditionally Cherubs were painted as angels with many wings and four faces: an ox, a human, a lion and an eagle. Each face represents a different aspect of that angel: The lion is representative of wild animals, but also strength and courage. The ox represents domestic earthly animals – or sentient beings. The human face represents humankind, and the eagle represents wisdom, spiritual vision, seeing things from a higher perspective, and birds. Often in ancient cultures, birds were representational of beings, which could walk between the spiritual realm and the earthly realm at will. The word Cherub comes from the Hebrew word Kerubh, which means winged angel.

The Cherubim are not plump-winged, little boys. Even Eros gets annoyed at being depicted like that. He says it's demeaning to who he is, and what he is capable of. The God of Love from the Greco tradition does NOT like being depicted like a Hallmark card. The Cherubim are ruled over by Raziel, who is the angel of divine thought. They work with your divine destiny and spiritual transformation. Cherubim are associated with the planet Uranus.

The Thrones

Zafkiel manages the Thrones; and he turns thoughts into ideas. They help protect us from dangers and obstacles, and are good angels to call on when you are undergoing challenges. Thrones are especially wise and channel divine wisdom to the world. They are associated with Saturn. The word Throne comes from the Latin root meaning to support or hold firmly. Call on the Thrones when you need support with your ideas, or want divine ideas, if you want help with the divine plan of goodness for your life, the divine plan of goodness for your relationships and the divine plan of goodness for your work.

Angels want us to invite them into our lives. They want you to ask them for help right now. When angels show up, miracles happen. I have seen amazing things happen consistently when you invite angel energy into your life.

Angel workout

What one thing would you ask the angels about the divine will for your life? What do you think is the divine will for your life? If you don't know, what would it be if you did know? Yes, just write down the first thing that comes to mind.

The Second Triangle:

The second triangle on the Tree of Life consists of love, strength and beauty. The archangels who govern these spheres are Zadkiel, Chamuel and Michael. On a physical level, this triangle represents your throat chakra, and your heart chakra. Michael rules the heart and the solar sun.

The Second Hierarchy of Angels:

The second group of angels are known as the angels of the cosmos, the regulative choir of angels who rule the universe, including all the galaxies, the multiverse; the entire cosmos. Many ancient cultures looked to the stars for divination, for navigation and for philosophizing about the meaning of life. On the Tree of Life, they also rule the world of creation. So once you have an idea or plan from the first hierarchy, now you meet the angels who will help you manifest your thoughts and ideas into a concrete form.

The Dominions

The Dominions originates from the Medieval word Latin dominio, and means sovereign authority. All leadership of created matter comes from the Dominions, who receive their instructions from the Thrones. If you think about it, a throne today means the seat of a King. Think of each group of angels as divine sovereigns who get their messages and instructions from divine source (or God), and they have a managing angel who rules over each group, then the entire group or choir of the angels above instruct the angels in the choir below.

The Dominions are associated with Jupiter and ruled by Angel Zadkiel. In the Kabbalah, the Dominions have been described as wearing long gowns, with exquisite golden belts, and they carry an orb or scepter. Angel experts say the Dominions govern the cosmos, they make order out of chaos and are channels for love and strength.

The Powers

The Powers are so called because they have divine power. They will help you refuse temptation and protect you from harm. The powers strengthen the good ascetics in spiritual struggles and labors, protecting them so that they may not be deprived of the spiritual kingdom. They help those wrestling with passions and vices. The Powers are associated with the planet Mars, and are ruled by Archangel Chamuel. Some traditions say Michael rules The Powers which makes sense to me as he is so powerful. I am following the system that was most common in my research.

Chamuel is one of my favorite angels. She is the angel of love and discernment, and rules the throat chakra. Zadkiel is the other Archangel who rules the throat chakra, and Archangel Michael rules the heart chakra. The Powers function mainly through your intuition, dreams or premonitions. They can warn you when danger is near.

The Virtues

The usual translation of the name of this order of angels as "virtues" is misleading if the old meaning of the word "virtue" as "power" or "force" is not remembered. The Virtues are filled with divine strength and quickly fulfill divine will. Michael is King of The Virtues. These angels are strong and powerful. Both The Powers and The Virtues work very great miracles and send down the grace of miracle-working to spiritual people, in order that they may work miracles, such as heal sickness and foretell the future. The Virtues help people laboring and those overburdened by tasks or jobs placed on them by someone, by which their name "Virtues" is explained and they bear the infirmities of the weak. They also strengthen your patience, so you do not crumble in crisis but face misfortune with a strong spirit, courageously.

The Third Hierarchy

These angels function as heavenly guides, protectors, and messengers to human beings

The Principalities

The Principalities are known as "Princedoms" and "Rulers", from the Greek word *archai*. Principalities are the angels that guide and protect nations, or groups of peoples, and institutions such as the Church. The Principalities preside over the bands of angels and charge them with fulfilling the divine ministry. There are some who administer and some who assist.

The Principalities are shown wearing a crown and carrying a scepter. Their duty also is said to be to carry out the orders given to them by the upper sphere angels and bequeath blessings to the material world. Archangel Haniel rules The Principalities. Think of her as the Queen of Love dispensing blessings where she goes and giving direction to the angels she rules to do so too.

Their task is to oversee groups of people. They are the educators and guardians of the realm of earth. They can inspire you to create great works of art or inventions. They will help you with business plans and creativity.

Archangels

An Archangel is an angel of high rank. Beings that are like archangels are many religious traditions and different cultures. The word archangel means chief angel. The archangels supervise the angels. Think of them like manager angels. The Archangels are ruled by Raphael and this live in the realm known as Hod.

Angels

Angels are considered the closest to the human realm whereas seraphim are considered closest to the godly realm. As you know angels are divine messengers and bright shining lights of divine energy. They are here to deliver messages, guide, comfort and help humans. There are seventy-two angels who you will meet in the next chapter. Each of these angels rules a different area. The angels live in Malkuth on the Tree of Life. Malkuth translates to The Kingdom. Uriel rules the angels. Some traditions say Metatron and Sandalphon are associated with the tenth sphere on the tree of life.

The tree of life is the western chakra system. In the Indian chakra system there are seven prominent chakras. The tree of life system incorporates the seven chakras' in the middle pillar and separates out the yin and yang forces into separate spinning wheels.

Angel workout

Think of the angel hierarchy as a ladder or stairway to heaven. Write any thoughts you may have below.

Have you ever practiced kundalini yoga?

DAY TWENTY. THE SEVENTY-TWO ANGELS

Did you know there are seventy-two angels who each govern four days a year, and twenty minutes each day? Different traditions and cultures talk about these angels.

They are known as the seventy-two names of God, the seventy-two angels of the Tree of Life, seventy-two emanations of divine source, and the seventy-two angels of the Kabbalah. They are in the book of Enoch in the Bible, and show up in many other traditions and cultures from ancient times. Each of these angels are governed by an angel who supervises them. Each correlate to a certain time of day, a few days each year and to a chakra and sephiroth on the tree of life. They are also known as the angels of astrology.

Western society has two forms of astrology. Most people have heard of their sun sign, Aries, Aquarius, Leo etc. But you may be unaware you have an angel who rules the day you were born and an angel who rules the time you were born. Like the zodiac year, angel astrology starts in March with angel Vehuiah who lives in Kether on the tree of life. Kether is ruled by Metatron, so Metatron supervises Vehuiah along with seven other angels. Metatron is the supervising or King angel of the Seraphim angel family. Think of astrological sun signs as different stages. Each sun sign carries its own energy.

Each Sephiroth carries its own energy too and there are ten stages we pass through each year, just as we pass through twelve sun sign stages. Sephiroth means emanation or spinning wheel of light as does the word chakra. Each angel that rules for four days has his or her own energy and attributes that blend well with their governing angel.

The governing angels are closest to God or divine source, and there are ten governing angels. These angels are in the chapters Ten Days of Archangels. Under each of these archangels are eight angels. Remember the angels are the closest level to the human realm. Each of these angel's rule for four days of the year, and for twenty minutes each day. Each angel also rules five different days on an emotional level, which will be explained below. To simplify this information, I have included a chart in this chapter so you can have easy access to which angel is your intellect and birth angel.

There are three angels that accompany each person

1.   Your angel guide
2.   Your heart angel
3.   Your mind or intellect angel

Your Angel Guide

Your angel guide is the angel who rules the day of your birth. This angel is with you all day, every day from the time you were conceived, till the time you pass over. It is his or her job to help you fulfill your divine life mission, and to help you navigate through the earthly plane. Your angel guide will have a quality which may help you with your life purpose. For example, my angel guide is Iahhel, and her name means "the desire to know". She rules January 26 to January 30th. Her aura color is turquoise, and the archangel who supervises her is Raphael.

Angel Iahhel looks like a mermaid angel, and the color of her aura, a sparkling turquoise, is very mermaid looking, or the color of a sparkling sea. Her job is to help with creativity and knowledge. She is the perfect angel for me, as ever since I was born, I have had a deep desire to know and to learn. My mother taught me to read at age three, and creative writing and English were always my strongest subjects. Plus, I love reading and swimming. I learned to swim when I was four, and at one time was considering becoming a professional swimmer. Instead I became a surf lifeguard when I was a teenager, and worked during summers when I was in college.

Each angel guide has their own aura color and strengths; you may find the angel who governs your birthday has traits you are strong in, or need help with.

Everyone has three main angels to call on, as well as their guardian angel.

You can also call on any one of the seventy-two angels who have the qualities you need help with any time. Angels can be in multiple places at the same time. They are not bound by the same physical laws that humans are. Ask the angels who have qualities you need help with to assist you today. Always remember there are Ten Archangels for you to call on. It is easiest to memorize the Ten Archangels first.

Your angel workout

Take a quick look at the angel chart and see which angel rules your birthday. Angel number one Is Vehuiah, and she starts ruling on March 21st to March 25th. This is because spring equinox occurs in the northern hemisphere on March 21st, which is also when the astrological calendar year begins with Aries. Does your angel guide have qualities you can relate to, or need help with?

Your Heart Angel

Your heart angel helps you on an emotional level. Each angel is also assigned five days a year to help people with their emotions. For example, angel Iahhel's heart days are May 23rd, August sixth, October 19th, December 29th and March tenth.

The angel who rules your heart and emotions, and his or her colors, are in the chapters on the archangels.

Your Intellect Angel

Each angel rules for twenty minutes every day. So Angel one, who is Vehuiah, rules from 12am to 12.20am. She is the angel of new beginnings and divine wisdom. The intellect time for my birth angel Iahhel (pronounced ee-ah-el) is from 8.20pm to 8.40pm. The time you were born determines who your intellect angel is. Some people have two. Your intellect angel helps you with mind matters and your heart angel helps you with emotional matters. Some people have two intellect angels. For example, I was born at 1pm, so I have two intellect angels:

Reheael (pronounced) Ray-ee-el, she is the angel of divine love. She rules from 12.40pm to 1pm and Yeiazel.

Angel Yeiazel (prounced Yaay-AH-Zel) rules from 1pm to 1.20pm. Since I was born at 1pm, and both Reheael and Yeiazel finish and start at one, this gives me two intellect angels to help me with matters of the mind. Yeiazel rules divine comfort and divine joy. Her name means divine joy or God is joy. She also strengthens the creative spirit, especially in design and writing. That explains why I chose writing as a career path. And this was way before I knew anything about the seventy-two angels.

I was ten when I started writing my first book. It was called Love in Los Angeles, and was going to be a romance. I loved reading Harlequin romances, so I always thought I'd be a romance writer. Interesting that my birth angel rules knowledge, and one of my intellect angels rule writing.

If you were born on the hour, you will have two intellect angels too. You will have two intellect angels if you were born at twenty minutes after the hour or twenty minutes before the hour.

Also, angel Yeiazel helps people who have anxiety and post-traumatic stress. She is the angel to call on when you are overcome with extreme struggle. She helps you become a hero or heroine ready to face any challenge, instead of being left feeling like a victim after a horrendous ordeal.

Remember you still need appropriate healing after going through a "trial by storm" period or dark night of the soul. But it helps knowing there are specific angels to call on for every life situation.

Angel Workout

Get familiar with the chart on the seventy-two angels. Write down your birthday angel and the Archangel who rules him or her. You will learn more about your birthday Archangel in the ten days of Archangels. You will learn more about the seventy-two angels in my book, Your Guiding Angel *which angel has your back?*

In 2015, I first began receiving messages from the angels to study the seventy-two angels, and write about them. I was going through my own crisis. I kept getting the message to write about the seventy-two angels, and that there are seventy-two thousand angels. Until Sunday I was wondering where the seventy-two thousand was coming from. I know new angels are being born all the time, just as new stars and planets and people are. I also knew on an astrological level, each sign rules for three thousand six hundred years. That is the same as the Mayan calendar. On Dec 21st of 2012, many people thought the world would end because it was the end of the Mayan calendar. What they didn't understand was that the new Mayan calendar began December 22nd 2012. We moved out of the age of Pisces, which had ruled for the past thirty-six hundred years, and into the age of Aquarius, which will rule for the next three thousand and 600 years.

In Māori tradition (the native people from New Zealand) Papatūānuku is the land. She is a mother earth figure who gives birth to all things, including people. Trees, birds and people are born from the land, which then nourishes them. Some traditions say that the land first emerged from under water. In the Māori creation story, Papatūānuku had many children with Ranginui, the sky father. Their children pushed them apart to let in the light. The children had more children, including birds, fish, winds and water. They became the ancestors of everything in the world today.

In Māori culture, there are seventy-two sons and daughters of Papatūānuku and Ranginui. Each son and daughter are a different aspect of divine source too. Many other cultures have three, six, nine, thirty-six, seventy-two and one hundred and eight as sacred numbers. This is interesting because twenty-seven has always been my favorite number (I am born on the 27th and this is an inversion of seventy-two). I kept wondering where I was getting seventy-two thousand from, because the angels were quite insistent this was important. I am part Māori, which is why I am using Māori traditions as examples. I kept writing stuff on Facebook, asking questions of my Māori friends to find out more information about the seventy-two sons and daughters of Rangi and the seventy-two angels. Finally, one of my friends wrote: *"Catherine, I think you are meant to make the connection and write about it!"* "Great," I thought. "How the hell am I going to do that?"

In November of 2016, as I was wrote this chapter, I was undergoing physio for a broken ankle. I managed to break two ankle bones, and fracture one other on July 5th, the day after Independence Day. While I was at the physio, my back went out. Richard, my physiotherapist, looked at MRI results for my back, and told me I had one vertebrae that was only partially attached near my fifth lumbar. This meant I could be extra flexible, but I needed to keep my spine strong to keep it stable.

I pulled out my old yoga book when I got home, to start my yoga routine again in earnest. I read the introduction, which I hadn't done in twenty years since I first bought the book. On page nine, there was a paragraph about the astral body (your spiritual body or higher self or inner being). It said: "Pranic Sheath: More subtle than the food sheath, but similar in form, it is often spoken of as the etheric double. It is made up of seventy-two thousand nadis, or astral tubes, through which prana, or vital energy flows." *Yoga Mind and Body by Yoga Vedanta Center, DK publishing 1996.*

Finally, I had found where the seventy-two thousand fit in. Then I wondered how many cells are in our body. Per my Google search, around thirty-six trillion, multiply that by two and you get seventy-two. Thirty-six, seventy-two and a hundred and eight are important numbers in many sacred traditions. Interestingly they are all derivatives of nine.

Below you will find your angel chart designed to help you discover your birth angel and your intellect angel.

The Seventy-Two Angel Chartw

The 72 angels

ANGEL NAME	QUALITIES	DAYS RULED	TIMES RULED	ANGELS, SEPHIROTH, AND COLORS RULED
				Archangel Metatron
1. Vehuiah	New Beginnings, Prosperity	March 21-25	12am – 12.20am	**Kether**
				Turquoise/Gold
2. Yeliel	Love, Wisdom	March 26-30	12.20am-12.40am	Red/Pink
3. Sitael	Expansion, Builder of Worlds	March 31-April 4	12.40am-1am	Pink/Red
4. Elemiah	Divine Power, Reparation	April 5-9	1am-1.20am	Orange
5. Mahasiah	Rectification, Facilitates Study	April 10-14	1.20am-1.40am	Violet/Deep Magenta
6. Lelahel	Divine Light	April 15-20	1.40am-2am	Emerald Green/Clear
7. Ahaiah	Patience, Understanding	April 21-25	2am-2.20am	Pale Blue
8. Cahetel	Divine Blessing	April 26-30	2.20am-2.40am	Violet/Pink
				Archangel Raziel
9. Hazayael	Divine Forgiveness	May 1-5	2.40am-3am	**Chokmah**
				Clear/Magenta
10. Aladiah	Divine Grace	May 6-10	3am-3.20am	Emerald Green/Pale Green

ANGEL NAME	QUALITIES	DAYS RULED	TIMES RULED	ANGELS, SEPHIROTH, AND COLORS RULED
11. Lauviah	Divine Victory	May 11-15	3.20am-3.40am	Violet/Gold
12. Hehaiah	Divine Refuge, Protection	May 16-20	3.40am-4am	Turuoise/Violet
13. Yezalel	Divine Allegiance	May 21-25	4.am-4.20am	Pale Green
14. Mebahel	Divine Truth/Justice	May 26-31	4.20-4.40am	Magneta
15. Hariel	Purification/Divine Witness	June 1-5	4.40am-5am	Pink/Violet
16. Hakamiah	Divine Loyalty	June 6-10	5am-5.20am	Purple/Burgundy
17. Laviah	Divine Motivation & Revelation	June 11-15	5.20am-5.40am	**Archangel Zafkiel** **Binah** Pale Turquoise
18. Caliel	Divine Justice	June 16-21	5.40am-6am	Purple/Pink
19. Leuviah	Divine Intelligence/Expanse	June 22-26	6am-6.20am	Purple/Clear
20. Pahaliah	Divine Redemption	June 27-July 1	6.20am-6.40am	Purple/Green
21. Nelahel	Desire to Learn	July 2-6	6.40am-7am	Turquoise/Pink
22. Yeyayel	Fame, Renown, Comfort	July 7-11	7am-7.20am	Pink/Gold
23. Melahel	Divine Healing	July 12-16	7.20am-7.40am	Pink/Pink
24. Haheuiah	Kindness/Protection	July 17-22	7.40am-8.am	Purple/Turquoise

ANGEL NAME	QUALITIES	DAYS RULED	TIMES RULED	ANGELS, SEPHIROTH, AND COLORS RULED
				Archangel Tzadkiel **Binah** Blue/Teal
25. Nithaiah	Divine wisdom & Magic	July 23-27	8am -8.20am	
26. Haaiah	Political Science & Ambition	July 28-2	8.20am-8.40am	Clear/Red
27. Yeratel	Propagation of the Light	Aug 2-6	8.40am-9am	Magenta/Turquoise
28. Seehaiah	Longevity	Aug 7-12	9am-9.20am	Green/Orange
29. Reiyel	Liberation	Aug 13-17	9.20am-9.40am	Royal blue/Lemon Yellow
30. Omael	Fertility/Multiplicity	Aug 18-22	9.40am-10am	Olive
31. Lecabel	Intellect/Talent	Aug 23-28	10am-10.20am	Turquoise/Clear
32. Vasariah	Clemency/Equilibrium	Aug 29-2	10.20am-10.40am	Pale pink/Pale Yellow
33. Yehuiah	Subordination to a Higher Order	Sep 2-7	10.40am-11am	**Archangel Chamael** **Sephiroth - Geburah** Blue/Clear
34. Lehahiah	Obedience	Sep 8-12	11am-11.20am	Orange/Violet
35. Khavakiah	Reconciliation	Sep 13-17	11.20am-11.40am	Green/Magenta
36. Menadel	Inner and Outer Work	Sep 18-23	11.40am-12am	Red/Green
37. Aniel	Breaking the Circle	Sep 24-28	12am-12.20am	Royal Blue/Gold

ANGEL NAME	QUALITIES	DAYS RULED	TIMES RULED	ANGELS, SEPHIROTH, AND COLORS RULED
38. Haamiah	Ritual and Ceremony	Sep 29-Oct 3	12.20am-12.40am	Gold
39. Reheael	Final Submission	Oct 3-8	12.40am-1pm	Red/Gold
40. Yeiazel	Divine Consolation/Comfort	Oct 9-13	1pm-1.20pm	Pale Yellow
41. Hahehel	Mission	Oct 14-18	1.20pm-1.40pm	**Archangel Michael Sephiroth - Tiphareth** Violet/Red
42. Mikael	Political Authority Order	Oct 19-23	1.40pm-2pm	Pale Yellow
43. Veuliah	Will, Prosperity, New Beginnings	Oct 24-28	2pm-2.20pm	Violet/Blue
44. Yelahiah	Karmic Warrior	Oct 29-Nov 2	2.20pm-2.40pm	Pale Yellow/Pale Pink
45. Sealiah	Motivation/Willfulness	Nov 3-7	2.40pm-3pm	Turquoise/Magenta
46. Ariel	Perceiver/Revealer	Nov 8-12	3pm-3.20pm	Rose Pink/Pink
47. Asaliah	Contemplation	Nov 13-17	3.20pm-3.40pm	Green/Gold
48. Mihael	Fertility/Fruitfulness	Nov 18-22	3.40pm-4pm	Gold/Clear
49. Vehuel	Elevation/Grandeur	Nov 23-27	4pm-4.20pm	**Archangel Haniel Sepiroth - Netzach** Pale Blue/Pale Yellow
50. Daniel	Eloquence	Nov 28-Dec 2	4.20pm-4.40pm	Blue/Red

ANGEL NAME	QUALITIES	DAYS RULED	TIMES RULED	ANGELS, SEPHIROTH, AND COLORS RULED
51. Hahasiah	Universal Medicine	Dec 3-7	4.40pm-5pm	Gold/Deep Magenta
52. Imamiah	Expiation of Errors	Dec 8-12	5pm-5.20pm	Blue/Orange
53. Nanael	Spiritual Communication	Dec 13-16	5.20pm-5.40pm	Pale Blue/Pale Pink
54. Nitael	Rejuvenation/Eternal Youth	Dec 17-21	5.40pm-6pm	Lilac/Pale Blue
55. Mebahiah	Intellectual Lucidity	Dec 22-26	6pm-6.20pm	Coral/Olive
56. Poyel	Fortune/Support	Dec 27-31	6.20pm-6.40pm	Clear/Turquoise
57. Nemamiah	Discernment	Jan 1-5	6.40pm-7pm	**Archangel Raphael Sephiroth - Hod** Pale Pink/Pale Blue
58. Yeialel	Mental Force/Love/Wisdom	Jan 6-10	7pm-7.20pm	Coral
59. Harahel	Intellectual Richness/Truth/Liberty	Jan 11-15	7.20pm-7.40pm	Pink/Clear
60. Mitzrael	Internal Reparation	Jan 16-20	7.40pm-8pm	Magenta/Clear
61. Umabel	Affinity Friendship	Jan 21-25	8pm-8.20pm	Red/Blue
62. Iah-Hel	Desire to Know	Jan 26-30	8.20pm-8.40pm	Turquoise
63. Anauel	Perception of Unity	Jan 31-Feb 4	8.40pm-9pm	Clear
64. Mehiel	Vivify/Enliven	Feb 5-9	9pm-9.20pm	Green/Blue

ANGEL NAME	QUALITIES	DAYS RULED	TIMES RULED	ANGELS, SEPHIROTH, AND COLORS RULED
				Archangel Gabriel **Sephiroth - Yesod** Coral/Turquoise
65. Damabiah	Fountain of Wisdom	Feb 10-14	9.20pm-9.40pm	
66. Manakel	Knowledge of Good & Evil	Feb 15-19	9.40pm-10pm	Yellow
67. Eyael	Transformation to the Sublime	Feb 20-24	10pm-10.20pm	Green/Red
68. Habuiah	Soul Healing	Feb 25-29	10.20pm-10.40pm	Pink
69. Reohael	DivineRestitution	Mar 1-5	10.40pm-11pm	Red/Deep Magenta
70. Yabamiah	Alchemy/Transformation	Mar 6-10	11pm-11.20pm	Yellow/Clear
71. Hayayel	Divine Mission	Mar 11-15	11.20pm-11.40pm	Blue/Violet
72. Mumiah	Endings and Rebirth	Mar 16-20	11.40pm-12am	Pale Violet

Angel Workout

Which angel rules the day you were born?

Which angel rules the time you were born?

Use this chart to call on specific qualities you would like help with. Ask the angel who rules those qualities to help you.

Remember each sephiroth has its own energy and we go through all the signs as stages as we cycle around each year. Sephiroths are emanations of energy or wheels of light like chakras and each angel is an emanation or aspect of God or Divine Source. So, put the word divine in front of each attribute.

DAY TWENTY-ONE.
ARCHANGEL METATRON

To bring Archangel Metraton's energy closer to you chant MET ARE TRON three times.

To bring any angel to you quickly chant their name three times with the best phonetic pronunciation you can. Hebrew and Aramaic are phonetic languages, as is Maori, they are sacred languages that have triple meanings and the pronunciation of the name is more important than the spelling as when you chant the name it sends the vibration out to the universe. The angel names were originally written in Aramaic.

Archangel Metatron:

Metatron is the go to angel for science, for math, for receiving divine information. He is the angel closest to divine source or God. Quantum physicists have been making giant leaps in their understanding of the Metatron's Cube, and the thirty-six trillion cells that govern our body. All our cells start out like the drawing of the Flower of Life from the time of conception when an ovum begins its life once fertilized.

Metatron's English name comes from the Latin *metator*: "one who metes out or marks off a place, a divider and fixer of boundaries," "a measurer", and Metatron is an archangel in the Jewish tradition, and is called the Recording Angel or the Chancellor of Heaven. How the name originated is often argued about. Metatron shows up mainly in sacred texts from the Kabbalah (book of knowledge). In that tradition, he is the highest of the angels, and serves as the celestial scribe or "recording angel". In the Christian tradition, Metatron appears in the book of Enoch as Sandalphon. Some traditions say Metatron was Sandalphon in human form, some traditions say he wasn't. Just as Christian denominations differ so too do angel traditions and beliefs.

Archangel Metatron is a good angel to call on for help with science and math, and writing, and studying, also for new inventions, for opening the crown chakra, for work, manifesting and life in general. He will help you reach your goals and plans. Metatron is the master manifestor of all the Archangels. He can open your spiritual senses, and your physical senses. He can help you break old patterns. Start afresh. Create a new life or a new relationship. He is the template builder of many things. Metatron is a powerful Archangel.

Some angel experts say he reaches all the way from earth to heaven, and builds a stairway (or bridge to heaven) and that he is extremely tall. I do see Metatron taller than most of the archangels when he shows up in my life.

Most of the Archangels show up to me as about ten feet tall, Metatron shows up as about fifteen feet, and the angels show up around seven feet. Remember, Angels are emanations of bright shining light, and when they show up in a human form people can recognize them because they look like a rainbow in terms of vibrancy, but appear differently to different people. "That's because all humans see things differently," say the angels. "Our energy is always pure and radiating our special qualities, but humans see us in different forms depending on their own upbringing, culture and personal beliefs. We don't mind how they see us, so long as they remember to call on us, that is the most important action."

Metatron's cube

To try to explain Metatron's cube in one paragraph is impossible, so I will give you a very basic explanation. Metatron's Cube is a sacred geometric symbol that forms a map of creation, and it is this 'map' that priests, mystics, 'enlightened ones' and ancient civilizations have revered throughout history. Scientists now are learning a lot more about Metatron's Cube, and how it relates to the creation of earth, and the creation of each human being.

Over thirteen billion years ago, during what is referred to on Earth as the 'big bang', Source (God, or Divine Intelligence) gave birth to our Universe. The symbol of Metatron's Cube explains this 'birth' and the infinite expanding field of Creation in all directions of time and space. This is a VERY basic understanding. There are tons of excellent books in the field, both in quantum physics and metaphysics, which can teach you more if you want to learn about it in depth.

Source energy, through the field of Metatron's Cube, creates the potential field of creation – a field of high vibrational frequencies that ripple out through creation eventually creating color, then sound, Archangels and angels, and finally at their lower levels of vibration – physical matter, which includes most of what we see on our planet.

Here is a picture of Metatron's Cube:

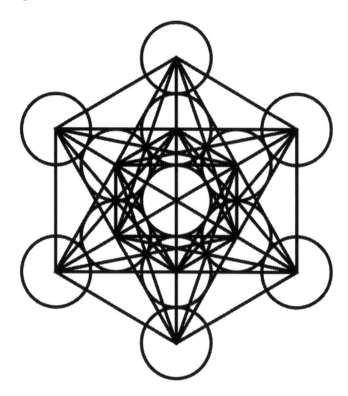

Image obtained from google search free usage rights.

Metatron's Cube is also called The Flower of Life

Have you ever watched The Flower of Life videos on the Spirit Science YouTube channel? They have some beautiful videos explaining a very complex idea into bite size chunks that are easy to understand. I have been drawing the Flower of Life since I was three. I did not know at the time that was what I was drawing. Whenever it was raining (which is quite a lot in New Zealand), I would get a piece of paper, a compass, a pencil and my crayons. Then I would sit at the kitchen table, and draw this design I thought I'd made up. I would draw two large circles to frame my drawing, then using my compass I would draw the flower of life with a pencil. Then using my crayons, I'd color in my Flower of Life, that I thought was just some pretty pattern. There is also the Fruit of Life, which some people believe is a metaphor for the fruit that Eve ate in the Bible.

In ancient Egypt, long before our modern religions, there were two mystery schools and thirteen pyramids where this subject originated. People spent twenty-one years training to become an initiate, or priest or priestess. Living a spiritual life has always required years of training; it is not for the faint-hearted. That's why I wrote this book in day-by-day pieces. My hope is that you will continue a spiritual practice every day for the rest of your life. In the Celtic tradition, warriors, druids and bards had to train for twenty-one years. Even the Dalai Lama has been in training since birth.

A quick aside, the Dalai Lama's birth name means "wish fulfilling goddess". Since I've been called Wish since I was four, I think I will start calling on "The Wish Fulfilling Goddess," maybe you could give it a try too. Making wishes is a fun magical tool to use that works. Kids do it all the time. Metatron says it is time for adults to start making wishes and daydreaming again too.

Metatron, Uriel and Sandalphon

Metatron rules the crown chakra, and there are some traditions that believe he rules the kingdom, which is a metaphor for earth as well as the crown chakra. Some traditions say Metatron is the only angel who was a person on earth, and that he was the brothers Uriel and Sandalphon. Other traditions say they are all three different emanations of divine source. No matter what tradition or culture, or whether Metatron rules the earthly realm as well as the crown chakra, Metatron, Sandalphon and Uriel all carry different energy and vibrations.

The Kingdom

The Kingdom in the Tree of Life is a metaphor for several things. It is a metaphor for the earth plane. It is a metaphor for the kingdom of heaven, our time on earth is meant to be spent creating heaven on earth. Although if you look around sometimes, it feels like people want to create hell on earth, internally with their own thoughts. And externally, with chaotic or argumentative relationships with friends and family, and globally with different countries and religions wanting to blow each other up or build walls of division.

I believe strongly the world is one big, giant blended family, and that we need to start treating it as such. A good book to read is "The Book of Joy" by the Dalai Lama and Archbishop Desmond Tutu. We need more joy both in our own lives and on the planet. Every day we are bombarded with images of violence and killing. It is important to remember what kind of media you consume. The media you listen to and watch daily feeds your mind. The nourishment you give your mind is just as important as the nourishment you give your body. For good mind nourishment music, check out Power Thoughts Meditation Club's channel on YouTube.

Metatron

Aura dark sparkling magenta, rich royal purple, violet
Sound – B, major, silence, and nnnnnnnnn – as in toning
Number - one
Gland - Pineal gland, hair, top of head, central nervous system
Crystals diamonds, clear quartz, selenite, kunzite

Essential oils lotus, lavender, calming serene oils, white rose oil
Chakra crown chakra,
Key word divine mind, divine will, divine source

Angels Metatron supervises from the seventy-two angels:

- Vehuiah
- Yeliel
- Sitael
- Elemiah
- Mahasiah
- Lelahel
- Ahaiah
- Cahatel

Tarot cards Metatron is associated with

- All the Aces, traditionally if an ace shows up in a reading, it means you are receiving a gift from God or from an unexpected source or divine source
- Ace of cups – soul love – a gift of love
- Ace of pentacles – prosperity, a gift of money
- Ace of swords – clarity, a gift of clear thinking
- Ace of wands – power and passion, a gift of help with a project or passion of yours
- The hierophant – faith
- The Priestess – carrier of great knowledge, someone who has been studying and practicing spirituality their whole life
- The Lovers – Archangel Michael brings joy and heart connection to lovers, Metatron adds a spiritual dimension to your relationship

Invocation
Angel workout:

"Dear Archangel Metatron, I invite you to embody me. I ask to carry your energy into the world today. I ask you to align my energy with yours. May I be a divine conduit of love and faith. Help me to trust divine spirit (or god) more and strengthen my faith. Open my crown chakra so I can receive divine guidance and divine messages easily. Lead me to the people, places and opportunities that will best help me. Strengthen my writing skills and learning ability."

Please help me with:

_____

_____

_____

_____

_____

_____

Please activate my dreams of _____

And protect me always with divine love and divine light

May your energy of love, understand, finding solutions help me with:

I ask for the highest outcome of all involved

And so it is

Amen

Thank you, Archangel Metatron"

Write about your experiences with Archangel Metatron below:

DAY TWENTY-TWO.
ARCHANGEL RAZIEL

To bring Archangel Raziel's energy to you chant Rah Tzee EL three times

Sometimes Raziel's name is also spelled Ratziel, and there are other spellings. But the important thing is to focus on is the phonetic pronunciation of all the angels, as well as chanting their names three times to bring their energy close to you.

Archangel Raziel and Archangel Zafkiel, who you will meet tomorrow, rule the brow chakra or the third eye. This spinning wheel of light is indigo, and is in the middle of your forehead. This is the seat of telepathy.

The brow chakra is also the place all ideas, inventions, songs, novels, plays, movies, and where business plans are thought up. Our imagination is our greatest gift, said Einstein, more important than knowledge. Einstein was right, because knowledge relies on knowing what has already been discovered, and learning about it. Imagination is the realm of magic where we can imagine new possibilities, new ways of thinking, new ideas. Walt Disney is one person who showed what is possible when we use our imagination. He turned an orange grove into Disneyland, and gave birth to a whole generation of movies. Disney is still one of the most successful movie making franchises.

Raziel's name means Divine thought, or wisdom, and Zafkiel turns thoughts into ideas. Your brow chakra is extremely important, and the way you use your mind is extremely important. Your mind is the seat of your self-image, the way you see yourself, the words you tell yourself, the way you see your future and where you can open to new possibilities. We all have several different probable futures depending on the decisions we make. Each day we are born again to create a new day, and our thoughts and actions determine not only our individual future, but collectively, the future of our planet. Planet earth is one big blended family divided by country boundaries and cultures and religions and political systems. When we individually use our own personal power, we can have a HUGE effect on what happens on a global level.

Have you ever noticed how each place has its own vibe? Like Albuquerque is desert land, hot searing sun, relentless in the summer, cold and dry in the winter. Sometimes the energy in Albuquerque feels harsh, as if there is a lot to break through. Plants are harder to grow, but it is also the land of enchantment, and many healers and authors, painters and creative people are led to New Mexico, Frieda Kahlo, Julia Cameron, Natalie Goldberg, Ottmar Liebert, Travis Tritt, Val Kilmer, to name just a few.

In California, the weather is more temperate, and each beach town along the coast has its own vibe. For example, Huntington Beach has a lot of mermaid energy everywhere, and has the vibe of Surf City, USA. People walk around in bikinis and swimsuits pretty much all year long. Los Angeles, the city of angels, is the entertainment capital of the world. Many great movies, records, bands, artist's careers have been launched in Los Angeles. The energy is always expanding and intense, because you have ten million people in a small area. Where you live is important, because you pick up the energy of the place and the people around you.

Archangel Raziel helps you think up new ideas, and open to new possibilities for your future. He will encourage you to expand your thinking of what is possible for your life. Call on Raziel when you want to clear out old ways of thinking and open your mind to a bigger, better, brighter future.

What we think about manifests, roughly in about six months' time.

Once I was in a situation where I kept saying: "I'm getting screwed over," until I did end up with a screw, literally, in my ankle. So be conscious where you place your thoughts. That is why meditation is so important. So often you might be busy during the day, and not have time to get still enough to listen to your intuition or divine messages. I find guided meditations help me the most. Yoga can be a form of meditation. For some people, sitting in a chair for twenty minutes might not be the best form of meditation, because you find your mind jumping all over the place. Putting on alpha music from YouTube will help your brainwaves slow down to about seven to fourteen counts per second, which is when you can receive divine messages.

Our analytical left-brain is always thinking, trying to solve problems, find solutions, or worrying about something. When you slow your brain waves down deliberately, and practice for fifteen minutes every day for a month getting into an alpha state, you can receive intuitive messages quickly, and also make a conscious choice in where you decide to put your mental focus.

If you are having trouble with obsessive thinking, ask Raziel for help. He can also help you design a new future, one filled with joy. This does not mean "bad" things will never happen. We come to the human realm to learn and grow; some of life's lessons are hard, and can be difficult to navigate through. We don't always have a choice in what happens to us, but we always have a choice on how to react. Ask Raziel for help in this area.

Archangel Raziel's sound: A major and OM

The angels from the seventy-two angels who Raziel supervises are:

- Hazayael
- Aladiah
- Lauviah
- Hehaiah
- Yezalel
- Mebahel
- Hariel
- Hakamiah

The tarot cards associated with Archangel Raziel are:

- All the twos (if you notice I have set up the Ten Days of Archangels to correspond to which sphere they dwell in on the tree of life, and which number they correspond to in numerology). Drop the twenty, and see what the second number is for a quick cheat sheet.

- two of pentacles – broadening your perception of what you can make financially
- two of swords – listening to your intuition to make a decision
- two of cups – new romance or friendship
- two of wands – travel
- All the knight cards. Knights are people cards, and can be either female or male even if the picture is a male. Knights represent emotional maturity of a young man or woman, and are not representative of the literal age although they can be

Crystals – amethyst, purple fluorite, sapphire, also emerald green and magenta are Raziel's colors

Essential oils: lavender, sage, peppermint, a drop of peppermint on your third eye is good for activating telepathy and clairvoyance

Both Raziel and Zafkiel direct the respiratory system, and the breath or "chi". Your respiratory system sends fresh oxygen to your blood every second. Spend some time every day taking deep breaths from your diaphragm; so often we can get caught up in shallow breathing. Close your eyes now and take three deep breaths, feeling your breath go all the way from your mouth down the bottom of your spine revitalizing every cell in your body with life-giving oxygen.

Call on Raziel too for help with lung, throat, flu, colds, pneumonia, asthma or any conditions associated with the throat or lungs. Both Raziel and Zafkiel will work together to help you with any conditions associated with the respiratory system, including toothaches, gum problems, and post-traumatic stress; that messes up your limbic system and fight or flight response.

Remember, your body cannot distinguish between what you are vividly imagining, and what is happening. If something triggers a memory or a flashback, your body may respond as if you are in that traumatic situation. Mixed martial artists, and many competitive sports players, know the importance of mental training. They use and train their mind just as much as they use and train their muscles. It is a good idea if you start today by training your mind to consciously focus on what you do want, instead of worrying about what you don't want.

Angel workout

"Dear Archangel Raziel, I invite you to embody me. I ask to carry your energy into the world today. I ask you to align my energy with yours. May I be a divine conduit of divine wisdom. May I radiate divine wisdom, and insight from my third eye throughout the day."

Please help me with:

_____

_____

_____

_____

_____

_____

Please activate my dreams of _____

And protect me always with divine love and divine light

May your energy of divine wisdom and clairvoyance help me with:

I ask for the highest outcome of all involved

And so it is

Amen

Thank you, Archangel Raziel"

Write about your experiences with Archangel Raziel below:

DAY TWENTY-THREE.
ARCHANGEL ZAFKIEL

To bring Archangel Zafkiel to you, chant Zaaaaf key El three times

There are variations on the spellings of these angels because they have been translated into English from Aramaic. Many angel names sometimes have T in front of them. For example, Zafkiel is also spelled Tzaphkiel. The angels say this is because British English is different from American English in pronouncing the letter Z. In Britain (and Canada, Australia and New Zealand) the letter Z is pronounced like 'zedd'. But in America Z is pronounced 'zee', so whenever you see an angel name starting with Tz, remember to pronounce it like 'zed' rather than 'zee'.

Archangel Zafkiel is the other angel who rules the brow chakra. In the Tree of Life, she is the Archangel who turns thoughts into plans; the action angel. Raziel envisions and dreams, while Zafkiel creates the business plan. Her aura is the most beautiful sparkling sapphire and turquoise, and she rules the mind and right eye. Raziel rules the left eye and the mind.

Zafkiel's key words are "turning thoughts into ideas", so once you have a thought, Zafkiel will help you outline a plan to execute the ideas. Her energy is moon-like and thoughtful. But she is also the "business" angel, or the architect of ideas. After you have a dream, an idea, want to improve your self-image, have an idea for an invention, a new business or New Year's goals ask Zafkiel for help in writing the ideas down onto paper, and formulating a timeline.

Every year I make an Angel Map. What is an angel map? It is a term I came up with one year, when I was tired of setting New Year's resolutions. New Year's resolutions for me usually consisted of:

1. Starting a diet
2. Upping my exercise plan
3. Writing four books
4. Increasing my clientele
5. Writing a marketing plan

And a whole bunch of other boring stuff that sounded like a lot of work. One year I heard Louise Hay talking about doing a New Year's meditation, and that sounded like a lot more fun than writing my HUGE to-do list.

I was also going to the Center of Spiritual Living in Albuquerque, and taking the foundations class with Reverend Patrick Pollard, learning lots of metaphysical techniques. So, I decided to combine them together and add a little angel energy. The result was an angel map – a map of navigating through your goals and dreams of the year.

Archangel Zafkiel is the perfect angel for helping you with this.

Angel Workout

Make your own angel map

How to make an angel map

1. Get a piece of paper and brainstorm some ideas
2. Allow yourself to get messy on paper
3. Call on Ratziel to help with ideas
4. Try to incorporate different areas of your life that are important to you
5. Family, health, romance, work, school
6. Think about where you'd like to be in a year from now
7. When you have an outline, open a word document, or use a blank piece of paper
8. Use my angel map below for inspiration or ideas
9. Type or write your map up

10. Laminate it – I usually make three copies, so I can post them around my home and office

Remember, it's okay to tweak your map throughout the year. For example, I did not complete everything on the angel map I made in 2016. I broke my ankle in July and had some other health issues come up, so everything had to get re-tweaked.

What I did accomplish was:

- Healing some chronic health conditions
- Learning how to walk again after having surgery and plates and screws inserted into my ankle
- Developed a healthy eating plan
- Developed a new exercise plan to help my broken ankle and strengthen my spine
- Finished two books, this one and one on beauty
- Took an online music business class for a semester through Berklee College of Music
- Started making notes for book four I am writing
- Learned about empathy fatigue and how to prevent it

Sometimes life happens, and we have to veer our boats in different directions. Yes, it sucks. I was not at all happy when my ankle broke. It totally changed the direction of the year. At the time, I was mad at the angels. Four months later I was thanking them. Having a broken ankle allowed me to focus on writing, get off social media, and take a break from everyone who was hitting me up with questions, which is really draining for people who have worked professionally as psychic life coaches. My doctor ordered me off social media so my body could get the rest it needed to heal, not just from the ankle, but also the post-traumatic stress.

Even though the intentions I had set for the year turned out differently, in the big picture, it was a much better scenario. I got to re-establish my career as an author, and start writing again.

You can also make an angel map with a blank piece of drawing paper and draw on it with pretty symbols, paint with water colors, sprinkle with glitter or cut pictures from magazines and make it fun. Like a vision board for your year.

The other qualities Archangel Zafkiel is good for help with is good fortune, happiness, richness, prosperity, law of attraction, faith, life coaching, divine guidance, improving your self-image, transforming adversity into strength (like with my ankle), clearing away feelings of unworthiness, help with any eye problems (especially your left eye), and also with the heart. Her and Archangel Michael can help you manifest a great love relationship. Together they rule the lovers in the tarot.

Since I went into the respiratory system in detail yesterday, and the sounds and essential oils for the brow chakra, I am not going to repeat that information again today.

The angels Zafkiel rules in the seventy-two angels

- Laviah
- Caliel
- Leuviah
- Pahaliah
- Nelahel
- Yeyayel
- Melahel
- Haheuiah

The tarot cards Zafkiel rules:

- All the threes, remember since this is day twenty-three, Zafkiel's number in numerology is three
- Three of swords – broken heart or disappointment
- Three of cups – celebration, girl time, fun, joy

- Three of wands - travel, growth, plans being accomplished, dreaming of something or someone far away
- Three of pentacles – conserving your money to invest into something worthwhile
- Zafkiel rules all the Queens in the tarot. The queens are emotionally mature, and have high emotional intelligence. On a chronological age level, women usually come into their sovereignty and queendom years around forty-five, meaning you get to rule your castle the way you want to
- Queen of Cups – someone who is artistic, sensitive and kind
- Queen of Swords – mental acuity, great clarity,
- Queen of Pentacles – smart business woman or great earth mother type figure
- Queen of Wands – fertility, active, accomplished projects, passionate, fiery

Invocation

"Dear Archangel Zafkiel, I invite you to embody me. That I may carry your energy into the world today. I ask you to align my energy with yours. May I be a conduit of your angelic energy of divine insight and action, and radiate divine joy to all people, places and _____(specific request)

Please activate my dreams of_____(specific request)

And protect me with divine love and divine light.

May your divine energy of _____(add your own request and prayers here)

I ask for the highest most benevolent outcome

Thank you, Archangel Zafkiel"

Angel workout for today:

"Dear Archangel Zafkiel, I invite you to embody me. I ask to carry your energy into the world today. I ask you to align my energy with yours. May I be a divine conduit of divine wisdom. May I radiate divine wisdom and insight from my third eye throughout the day."

Please help me with:

_____

_____

_____

_____

_____

_____

Please activate my dreams of _____

And protect me always with divine love and divine light

May your energy of divine wisdom and clairvoyance help me with:

I ask for the highest outcome of all involved

And so it is

Amen

Thank you, Archangel Zafkiel"

Write about your experiences with Archangel Zafkiel below:

DAY TWENTY FOUR.
ARCHANGEL ZADKIEL

To bring Zadkiel close to you chant ZAD KEY EL three times.

Archangel Zadkiel's aura is a beautiful emerald green and soft pink, like the colors of the heart chakra, even though she rules the throat chakra along with archangel Chamuel.

Both Zadkiel and Chamuel can help with matters of the heart, as well as matters of the mind, and articulate a way to express them. They dwell in the realms where form becomes matter, where ideas and desires from the imagination take tangible form in the expression of brainstorming, like business plans, and then Zadkiel and Chamuel can help you manifest them, or carry out the plans.

Zadkiel is like the empress, and rules the universe. She oversees the nurturing of our planet. Her heart overflows with divine love and mercy. Her energy is like the Goddess Kuan Yin.

Her symbols:

The Vesica Pisces
The Earth
White lotus, Kuan Yin and White Tara are also associated with this beautiful flower and essential oil
Pink roses, my favorite (especially sweet-smelling ones). The pink of Zadkiel is the color of soul love, whereas magenta is Chamuel's other aura color. Zadkiel's is emerald.

Zadkiel rules the right arm, (or your dominant arm), so she is the angel to call on when you want to project and radiate love and compassion from your hands. Our hands have chakras, and we can use them for so many things. We use them to write, to create, to paint, to build, to brush our hair, to hold our children, pat our animals, pick flowers. To enwrap a loved one in a HUGE hug, to hold a lover's face in our hands and gaze into their eyes, for cooking dinner, cutting vegetables and for laying on of hands healing. These are all ways that you use your right hand to broadcast love through your astral cells and hand chakras (spinning wheels of light).

Our hands are VERY important say the angels. This is why palm reading was so prevalent in the 1920s. Our hands project and receive energy, so we need to keep their energy fields clean, the hand chakras spinning brightly and to be aware of what kind of energy we are sending out. Every emotion we feel is being broadcast into whatever we use our hands for, whether that is giving someone a massage, hitting something, stroking someone's back, doing housework or cooking.

Our hands are powerful, say the angels. That is why palmistry is such an old divination method. Our hands tell a story. To clear the hand chakras, wash your hands, and moisturize them with hand cream, coconut oil, rose oil or lavender. Then rub both hands together for fifteen seconds. And be conscious how you use your hands throughout the day. Our eyes and hands project energy; our ears and left hands receive energy. Since Chamuel rules the left side of the body, she can help more with receiving messages, whereas Zadkiel will help more with sending messages.

Both Zadkiel and Chamuel work together to help you will all matters of vocal expression.

My son Kylan says he likes Archangel Zadkiel a lot. I asked him why, and he said: "I really like her divine feminine nature."

My son Kylan said he was calling on Zadkiel a lot recently to help him balance out his masculine and feminine side, to balance his right and left brain, the sun and moon energy within him, and the fire and water.

He said Zadkiel has been helping him. Funny, I didn't know Kylan knew about Zadkiel!

Kylan was featured in Doreen Virtue's Crystalline Children (Hay House) book. The book closed with him saying: "I want people to know the earth has a heart, and that people should make signs and stick them on their wall. The signs should say "Be Happy!"

My son is way more psychic than me. I have two sons, Logan and Kylan. They grew up with a mom who is a free spirit, who talked to angels, who taught law of attraction classes, built a music company (that is a whole other book!), and made them listen to Tony Robbins, Napoleon Hill, Dale Carnegie, Louise Hay, and Wayne Dyer since they were born. They poo-pooed my metaphysical beliefs and teachings when they were teenagers. As adults Kylan has surpassed me. when I was offered an opportunity to speak at a Hay House event, Kylan wanted to go to see Gregg Braden speak. I guess he gets to hear me speak every day!

Zadkiel is the angel who will bring you good fortune, happiness, and prosperity in all areas of your life; she will help lift your spirits when you feel down. She will teach you how to speak words that empower you, instead of words that criticize you, both in your self-talk, and when you are speaking to others.

Zadkiel says too many people use words carelessly, and are very unkind to themselves in their thoughts and their words. She says call on her to improve your speech, because what you say matters. What you say today will create a spiritual blueprint to go out into the spiritual universe, and show up in your life in six month. If you are constantly saying (or thinking): I'm too fat, I'm too broke, I'm too overwhelmed, chances are you will be fat, broke and overwhelmed six months from now.

Zadkiel also says she can help you change the way you see yourself, because sometimes people think they are too fat or not good enough, defined by some silly human expectation. Your view can get distorted. She will help you with right thinking. Zadkiel has kind, loving, mother earth energy. She will always feed you and love you.

Archangel Zadkiel:

Aura Pale green and pastel pink
Sound – G, major, HAM
Gland - Thymus
Crystals rose quartz, rose sapphire, emerald, any pale pink or pale green stone
Essential oils lotus, water lily, honey suckle, pink roses, rose,
Chakra throat chakra,
Key word understanding
Angels she supervises from the seventy-two angels:
Nithaiah
Haaiah
Yeratel
Seehaiah
Reiyel
Omael
Lecabel
Vasariah

Tarot cards she is associated with

The World -The World represents an ending to a cycle of life, a pause in life before the next big cycle beginning again with The Fool. It teaches us it is good to give back to The World
Death - change, transition
The chariot – movement - progress
The wheel of fortune – change for the better
The emperor – good business man, business matters,
Four of wands – marriage
Four of swords - meditation
Four of pentacles – being thrifty
Four of cups – sulking over what is lost when something better is on its way
The number four in numerology is about

Angel workout:

"Dear Archangel Zadkiel, l I invite you to embody me. I ask to carry your energy into the world today. I ask you to align my energy with yours. May I be a divine conduit of love and understanding. Help me speak my truth and see myself clearly. May I radiate divine courage and encouragement from my heart center and think it and speak it throughout the day."

Please help me with:

_____
_____
_____
_____
_____
_____

Please activate my dreams of _____

And protect me always with divine love and divine light

May your energy of love, understand, finding solutions help me with:

I ask for the highest outcome of all involved

And so it is

Amen

Thank you, Archangel Zadkiel"

Write about your experiences with Archangel Zadkiel below:

DAY TWENTY-FIVE.
ARCHANGEL CHAMUEL

To call Chamuel's energy to you chant Sha arm you el three times

Her name means "throne of god", "divine throne" or "divine rule"

Chamuel is the archangel of love, strength and judgement. She is my birthday Archangel, and the first time I saw her was when I was three. She appeared by my bed with her long flowing blonde hair in a white gown with an aura the most beautiful color of pink. The color of soul love. Angels show up as personification, so humans can identify them.

Archangel Chamuel and Archangel Zadkiel rule the throat chakra together.

Archangel Chamuel rules the throat chakra, allowing you to communicate clearly. She is a great Archangel for lovers, for writers, for romantics, for empaths and lightworkers. She is good at helping people to strengthen their boundaries, and not give your precious life energy to someone else's dreams, visions and desires, but to focus on your own. Chamuel has saved me from this in many situations. Most lightworkers love helping others, or spend hours trying to save people or invest their time, energy and resources into other people gladly. Chamuel is adamant that it is time to STOP. Lightworkers and empaths run the risk of getting empathy fatigue, Chamuel says.

These are the old ways of the Age of Pisces, where the energy was about self-sacrifice for another's needs. This new Age of Aquarius, she says, is about having a new vision, a new way of thinking, a new perspective. She encourages change, and easy transitions. She can be quite blunt when you are talking to her, but her messages always come in waves of love.

One day, years ago, I was talking to her in my head as I walked from my car towards the grocery shop in Albuquerque. I was feeling nostalgic, and still grieving the loss of a long-term relationship.

"Maybe we could get back together?" I asked Chamuel and the angels under her.

I no sooner sent out the thought then I got whacked in the head by a four by two piece of wood sticking out of someone's car. I landed on my back and had a slight concussion. People in the parking lot were running to help me. Chamuel and her team and my guardian angel whacked some sense into me with a wooden log. The angels can be quite literal sometimes. Especially when you are ignoring their advice after requesting it or trying to reason with them. Or if they don't think it's for the highest and best outcome for everyone involved.

Empaths and kind-hearted people are at risk for being targets for emotional predators. These guys (or women) know what they are doing. They do not fall in love. They look for targets, people they can resource. They have low levels of remorse and low levels of empathy. They fake emotions, and they are chameleon in that they become whatever you want them to be. They paint a picture of how wonderful a future with them will be like. But they only occasionally give you something they say they are going to. They groom you when you first meet them by love bombing you, appealing to your good nature, and playing upon your insecurities. They listen and observe, so while you are falling in love, they are plotting behind the scenes to come up with their big con. They are the ultimate con artists. They use the same techniques that cult leaders, religious zealots and some politicians use.

If you have had a history of being in relationships where you are always giving or being mistreated or falling in love with someone's potential, Chamuel will help you choose wisely.

A high tolerance to neglect means you are used to spending a lot of time on your own, and often enjoy your own company. This gives them license to exploit you, and not tend to the relationship. Or you may come from a family where you were ignored a lot, or have been ignored or shy when you were young. You may feel guilty when asking for things for yourself, even things like birthday presents, spending a week away together, or just time in general. You may feel guilty saying no.

Sociopaths are master manipulators and when they are love bombing you, they will pull out the red carpet and all the stops with great promises of the future. But once they've sucked you into the relationship, this changes to power and control. They resource you and exert power over you, at the same time using clever manipulation techniques, so you wind up feeling as if you are the crazy one or that everything is your fault, or you have major depressive episodes, and don't know why. You are not the crazy one. Your response is normal. Being with an emotional predator is draining, dangerous and depressing, they are extremely good at resourcing, manipulating, pathological lying, and knowing which buttons of yours to make you feel bad about yourself.

They hold out the proverbial carrot to keep you hanging on to the relationship. Loyalty is a noble quality that is often lost today. Insane loyalty is where you are loyal to the t that you are compromising your own values. You may have empathy fatigue. You may be putting up with bad behavior. If so, consider getting out. For example: putting up with cheating, a partner going missing for long periods of time, being criticized harshly or ridiculed or being devalued in any way, being continually lied to, hit or stolen from. If you have been hurt physically by your partner get help. Talk to a trusted professional. You can work out a safety plan without telling anyone and keep it until you feel it is time to leave.

Leaving any situation and going through a major transition is painful, scary and uncertain. Uncertainty can raise a lot of feelings around finances, places to live, practical matters, as well as bringing up your own insecurities and fears.

Archangel Chamuel rules transition. She is the angel of the number five, which is all about transition, and the fear and excitement that accompanies it. When change is going on in your life ask Chamuel for help. She will make the transition as smooth as possible, and help with the grieving or emotions you are experiencing. She can also help you alter your thinking about the change. If you are thinking the change is "bad", she will help you see the good in it, she will show you the situation from her spiritual experience and give you peace of mind. She will also help you ask for what you need.

Once I had a friend who was dear to my heart. We had a fall-out due to a major miscommunication. We were both horribly hurt. The next day he said he needed some space. We were working on a project together, so I had to finish the project alone. I experienced all kinds of grief emotions that I couldn't articulate. Once again, I was mad at the angels.

"Why did you bring him into my life, if you were on going to take him out so soon?" I whined.

Two months later (after asking Chamuel and many other angels for help) I received a message that he would be in touch when the time was right.

This time, I had been asking for a lot of angelic assistance. He is someone dear to my heart. What happened was a misunderstanding that hurt both of us deeply. Sometimes soul connections are hard to navigate. My belief is that soul relationships cause our souls to grow and stretch and this can be painful at times. I am happy to say our relationship deepened because of our misunderstanding. But it took work, forgiveness, self-reflection, prayer and meditation as well as action.

Chamuel will help you make major decisions, transition with more ease and grace, be more discerning, and not so willing to trust immediately when someone new shows up in your life. She is the street-smart angel. The archangel with a kind, loving heart who will help you articulate with wisdom, strength and kindness the most beautiful words possible for any situation, including writing a message where you are experiencing tricky emotions like anger, frustration, or betrayal, as well as with the kind emotions like compassion and forgiveness -although those are more Zadkiel's domain.

Archangel Chamuel can help you make wise choices in daily matters too. For example, this morning I woke up and wanted to jump on Facebook. Chamuel gently advised me to start writing on this instead. "You will get lost in Facebookland for two hours," she said. "That's two hours of lost writing time. I will help you with your writing, if you open your word document instead of Facebook." Ask Chamuel for help making wise choices in big matters and little matters today.

Archangel Chamuel champions for kind-hearted people and empaths. She knows the challenges we face and how trusting we can be.

Archangel Chamuel:

Aura sparkly pink and magenta
Color like the pink in a rainbow – the color of soul love
Sound – G, major, HAM
Gland/physical areas hearing, left arm, limbic system.
Chamuel says to call on her for help with easy transitions, re-setting your nervous system and balancing your limbic system, especially normalizing your fight or flight response if you have been in any trauma. She will comfort you, help you speak up and deal with throat problems. She can teach you about energy fatigue and how to prevent it. This is an essential skill for empaths.
Crystals rose quartz, ruby, amethyst, turquoise, aquamarine, sapphire, sodalite, wear colors of her aura or crystals to bring her close to you
Essential oils gardenia, honeysuckle, white frangipani, rose, patchouli
Chakra throat chakra,
Key word listen, discernment, empathy fatigue prevention

Angels she supervises from the seventy-two angels:

- Yehuiah
- Lehahiah
- Chavakiah
- Menadel

- Aniel
- Haamiah
- Rehael
- Yeiazel

Tarot cards:

- Five of swords – the five cards in the tarot are tricky because they deal with extremes. Five of swords is someone could be deceiving you or having mixed thoughts about a situation or person
- Five of wands -building together in unison, or a complete mess with everyone fighting
- Five of cups – disappointment, grief, turn around and focus on the two cups left standing – put your energy towards that
- Five of pentacles – fear or faith
- Ten of wands – victory, accomplishment or feeling overwhelmed and carrying the load for everyone
- Ten of cups – happy families, prosperity on all levels
- The magician – the magician has all the tools he needs and he brings forth ideas from the realm of our imagination into tangible form
- The star – dreams and desires coming true, wish upon a star, pouring love and compassion to the world, the wish fulfilling goddess, love, beauty and wisdom

Angel workout

"Dear Archangel Chamuel, I invite you to embody me. I ask to carry your energy into the world today. I ask you to align my energy with yours. May I be a divine conduit of peace, compassion and discernment. May I radiate divine love and speak from my heart center throughout the day."

Please help me with:

_____

_____

_____

_____

_____

_____

Please activate my dreams of _____

And protect me always with divine love and divine light

May your energy of courage, strength and compassion help me with:

I ask for the highest outcome of all involved

And so it is

Amen

Thank you, Archangel, Chamuel"

Write about your experiences with Archangel Chamuel below:

Write about ways you may be experiencing empathy fatigue and how Chamuel can help you. Chamuel is insistent we must educate ourselves about empathy fatigue to avoid burnout

DAY TWENTY-SIX.
ARCHANGEL MICHAEL

To bring Archangel Michael's energy to you chant his name MEE KAY EL three times

Archangel Michael is the archangel who rules the heart chakra.

His aura colors are yellow and blue

His name means "like God" or like Divine energy.

Michael shows up in a lot of different religions and cultures. In Roman Catholic, Eastern Orthodox, Anglican, and Lutheran traditions, he is called "Saint Michael the Archangel" and "Saint Michael". In the Oriental Orthodox and Eastern Orthodox traditions, he is called "Taxiarch Archangel Michael" or simply, "Archangel Michael".

Michael rules the heart chakra. He is one of the few archangels who have solo dominion over a chakra, most of the chakras have two angels. On the Tree of Life, the chakra Michael rules is Tiphareth, the spinning wheel of divine light and divine beauty. Michael is known as the closest angel to God or divine source.

Michael talks to me a lot about courage. I asked him how he got to rule the heart chakra, since he is most known for being the bodyguard angel with his band of mercy, where he wields a flaming sword with blue flaming light, the same color as blue gas flames. He says because he is the angel closest in vibration to the energy of divine source, or like God. He is also considered the heart of man on the tree of life.

That's why he rules the heart. Scientists are finding out now that the heart center rules the body, whereas before they thought the brain ruled the body. The heart is the center of our body. Our emotions give fuel to our thoughts. Our thoughts might be the realm where creation takes place. This is where we send out thought waves into the universe, where they are recorded in the Akashic records, then show up in our lives about six months later. I am talking about your most predominant thought forms. These are ruled by the angels who rule the brow chakra, Raziel and Zafkiel. The throat chakra is ruled by Zadkiel and Chamuel; and Michael is the sole angel who governs the heart. Other angels help him, so don't think you can only call on Michael for help with matters of the heart.

When I asked Michael why he was given the heart to rule, because the heart chakra is in the beautiful spinning wheel of beauty, and harmony and compassion in your physical heart region, spreading down your torso, he said five things:

1. He helps humans protect their hearts
2. He helps humans deal with things that hurt their hearts, be they physical things like over exertion, high blood pressure, cigarette smoking or eating fatty foods. As well, he helps humans protect their heart on an emotional level.
3. He encourages your heart's desires
4. He raises your level of courage
5. He helps you live from your highest self to be more "Godlike" or Divine.

Courage and love work together for your greatest good.

Archangel Michael is the go-to angel for helping heal addictions. He will use his flaming blue sword to cut away etheric cords that keep you bound to an addiction.

The heart is associated with the word courage, says Michael.

The word courage comes from Old French *corage* "heart, innermost feelings; temper," from Vulgar Latin coraticum (source of Italian *coraggio*, Spanish *coraje*), from Latin *cor* "heart."

It is a common metaphor for inner strength. In the middle ages courage was used broadly for "what is in one's mind or thoughts", not only bravery, but also wrath, pride, confidence, lustiness, zeal and strength.

The heart not only physically rules the body center, it rules your emotional heart and innermost feelings, and as you see above, inner strength and what's in your mind. Heartmath foundation has done a lot of studies on the heart. These studies show what you think about changes the strength of the heart waves you emit. These waves can be measured and are powerful because this is the energy you are sending out.

Heartmath discovered people know two to three seconds before something happens what will happen. Visit Heartmath's website to learn more.

Your mind and thoughts affect your heart. Your emotions give volition or fuel to whatever you are thinking about. Archangel Michael whose aura is blue like a gas flame, and yellow like sunshine, can help you have courage, be brave, develop inner strength, as well as protecting you and assisting you to break free from any addictive behavior, whether it is a substance or an addictive pattern like workaholism, eating disorders, gambling addiction, or a substance addiction.

Addictions wreak havoc on people's lives and their loved ones. Many addicts also have

mental health challenges or began using to self-medicate their pain.

Lightworkers beware, unless you are a trained professional, you cannot afford to be around the energy of an addict. Addict energy is draining, chaotic and takes a lot of your energy and personal power. I have met many lightworkers who want to "help" addicts. This is dangerous territory especially for people who are highly empathetic or sensitive to energy as most lightworkers are. Turn addiction problems over to Archangel Michael and stay away from addict energy.

Drug addicts can be extremely good manipulators, and many lightworkers are not very street smart. Addicts often manipulate kind-hearted people in to get a fix. Whether you are giving them money for food, or a place to live, Archangel Michael is adamant this is not the territory for lightworkers. He says to remember when you try to help an active addict, their money often ends up in the hands of gangs, and these gangs have no mercy when it comes to murdering people, including women and children. What you might think is helping someone, may very well be killing someone else. Addicts put you at extreme risk of developing empath fatigue and this can kill you. The angels are adamant we must learn about empathy fatigue and take daily steps to prevent it.

Encourage is another word associated with the heart chakra and Michael. Encourage is from Old French *encoragier* "make strong, hearten". Michael will encourage and motivate you to use your time and personal power wisely. To invest in your dreams, desires and things that will move your life forward. He will help you say "no" when other people are trying to get you to give them more energy than is healthy. He is a loving, but direct angel.

The suffixes of angel's names are important. In classical Hebrew from which the Bible was first translated after Arabic, "-el" stands for God/Lord/Power in Hebrew. "El" means "God" or "Power" in Hebrew. It is a common element in many names in the Bible, and in the modern Hebrew language. Because of the major influence that the Bible had on many cultures, such names became common in languages like French, Russian, English, German and others. It is commonly read as either "of God" or "God is" in names, but there are many different other semantics possible, too.

El was the name of God of the northern Israelite tribes, while the southern tribes tended to use names that began with *"Jo"* such as Joseph, or end with *"-iah"* e.g. *Isaiah, Ezekiah, Adonijah,* Josiah. That is why many angel names end with either -el or -iah. The translation over time from Aramaic, Biblical Hebrew, sometimes called Classical Hebrew, is an archaic form of the Hebrew language. The very first translation of the Hebrew Bible was into Greek.

The first major translation of the Bible into the English language did not happen until the Middle Ages. The Tyndale Bible, named after the priest who translated it, was first published in 1526. This is why when you see angel names sometimes they have different spellings like Zafkiel, Tzaphkiel, Chamuel or Cassiel. There are many variations of spellings into English from the original Aramaic. I have tried to write the angels; names in the easiest way to pronounce in English. The phonetic pronunciation is more important than the spelling. When you chant any angels name three times it automatically calls that angel to you.

The angels that Michael supervises:

Hahehel
Mikael
Veuliah
Seliah
Ariel
Asaliah
Mihael

The tarot cards associated with Archangel Michael are:

The lovers – Archangel Michael is shown in all his glory protecting the hearts of the lovers
King of Pentacles – a great business man
King of Swords – a great thinker
King of cups – an emotionally mature man, someone interested in the arts
King of Wands – a leader, a successful entrepreneur
Six of swords -travel, rescue,

Six of Cups -happy memories, children, contentment,
Six of wands – victory, leadership, success
Six of pentacles – gifts, charity work, divine help
Six in numerology is stability, level headed, nurturing

Michael carries similar energy to the legend of King Arthur. He has very male, very golden energy. And he is a good angel to call on for leadership advice. He rules the heart, the torso and the circulatory system. Your circulatory system is very important. It lies the closest to your soul and is the heart of your life. Archangel Michael ensures that all thirty-six trillion cells in your body get a fresh supply of oxygen and nutrients every second of your life.

Call on Michael to purify and enliven your bloodstream. Ask him to clean your arteries, regenerate your cells, activate your thymus gland and strengthen your immune system. If you imagine archangel Michael filling all thirty-six trillion cells with divine light and divine love each morning or evening, that is the best wrinkle cream you can use. He will help your cells regenerate and revitalize and keep them healthy and bright.

I have always experienced Michael as a very masculine, active, yang energy. His energy is strong and powerful like the solar sun. He radiates golden light.

Angel workout:

"Dear Archangel Michael, I invite you to embody me. I ask to carry your energy into the world today. I ask you to align my energy with yours. May I be a divine conduit of peace, compassion and harmony. May I radiate divine courage and encouragement from my heart center throughout the day."

Please help me with:

_____

_____

_____

_____

_____

_____

Please activate my dreams of _____

And protect me always with divine love and divine light

May your energy of courage, strength and compassion help me with:

I ask for the highest outcome of all involved

And so it is

Amen

Thank you, Archangel Michael"

Write about your experiences with Archangel Michael below:

DAY TWENTY-SEVEN. ARCHANGEL HANIEL

To bring Haniel to you immediately chant HAH NAY EL three times

Archangel Haniel is the sister angel to Raphael on the Tree of Life. Together they rule the solar plexus chakra located in your upper tummy region. This chakra is bright yellow, and the key words are thoughts logic and personal power. This is the region of your inner sunlight, the place of your personal power.

Tomorrow, you will meet Archangel Raphael, who is known for his healing abilities. He helps Haniel work with you on personal power, and the way you see yourself. Raphael rules the left leg, while Haniel rules the right leg. Metatron rules the whole body and the feet. He keeps you grounded, as well as opening your mind to new ideas and a new vision for your life.

Archangel Haniel sparkles with divine light. Her aura is a beautiful opal color. She is an angel of peace, serenity and love.

She can help you find deep levels of love within yourself. She will remind you to focus on the solution, rather than the problem, so you can turn the energy of action into a new fresh direction. Because she is the Archangel of serenity, inner peace and healing trauma, she is a great angel to call on if you have experienced deep trauma or been through a life-changing incident. She will help you forgive when the time is right. But mostly she will help you heal, and be kind to yourself and grant you serenity and peace of mind. Call on her if you suffer from anxiety or panic attacks.

Haniel will help you heal emotionally and mentally, and Raphael will help you heal physically. She will help any problems you may have with your family, your friends, your children or your beloved. She is the go to angel for relationship problems, and will willingly listen for hours on end if you need someone to talk to. She can help you express your feelings and find the right words to speak up in matters of love.

Haniel can help you appreciate beauty and harmony, and help with creative projects. Love, beauty and wisdom are her domain, and Venus is the planet she is associated with. Venus is the goddess of love, beauty and wisdom in ancient Roman mythology.

Call on her too for happiness and a soul love relationship. She can help you turn your fortune into good luck and help your talents to blossom.

Haniel is a beautiful archangel, and her nature is very feminine, her energy is kind and loving, gentle and serene. She will help you connect with your divine nature, your spiritual or higher self. She is also the angel of awareness. She is one of the five Archangels who can help you with love magic.

Main Angels of Love Magic

The five main Archangels of love magic are Haniel, Michael, Gabriel, Raphael and Uriel. Within the seventy-two angels, there are other angels who can help you with different qualities of love. Call on these angels to assist you with love, romance and happiness.

Call on them for matters concerning your home. Five is the number of change, it is the number of Archangel Chamuel, and it is also the number of divine source or spirit depending on your tradition. Six is the number of harmony, compassion and nurturing. People born with six as their birth number in numerology are natural caregivers. When taken to extreme this can lead to rescuing people in distress or mothering adults who don't want to grow up or empathy fatigue. Chamuel and Haniel work well together so you find balance.

Haniel rules love, harmony, affection, peace and harmony.

She is the go-to angel for your feelings about your sexuality, and attractiveness. Haniel will help you find a balance between personal grooming, exercise, health and wellbeing. She will help you create beauty, beauty is an ideal that can be created. Just ask any self-respecting French woman. Haniel can help you if you have feelings for someone, and want to know how they feel about you. She will help you create balance between liking someone, and knowing you are the queen of your own castle.

Too often at the start of a relationship, we give a lot of time and energy to the relationship. This is important in the process of getting to know someone, but you always want to be the sovereign of your land. What does this mean? Think of your land as a metaphor for your home, your food, your assets, your dreams, your goals. Think of all the things you rule. Make a list of them:

For example, a list might look like this;

I _____ rule:

- ♥ My home
- ♥ My body
- ♥ My time
- ♥ My mind and emotions
- ♥ My health
- ♥ Where my time, energy and resources go
- ♥ How I plan my day and invest my time
- ♥ Where I want to live and who I want to hang out with
- ♥ The kind of foods I eat

Use that as a template, but create your own list. You will find you govern different things at different times. Five years ago, I was raising two teenage sons, had a psychic reading business in Albuquerque, and was in process of getting divorced. That list looked a lot different than my list today.

What do I rule?

Always remember you are the sovereign of your own land, and you get to reign in the way that you wish. Do not fall in love with someone's potential. Do not invest more time, energy and money into other people than you do into yourself. Do not put other people in front of yourself. This is not being selfish; this is practicing good self-care. Kind hearted people tend to be super generous often at the expense of their own health. You can run yourself ragged putting other people's needs ahead of your own. This is empathy fatigue. If you do it continuously, you will get sick.

Call on Haniel if this has been one of your patterns. She will help you find the balance between love and compassion for other people, and love and compassion for yourself. She will encourage you to extend the same generosity as you do to other people to yourself, without feeling guilty. In fact, you will feel happy that you are taking good care of yourself and setting good boundaries, because then you will have more energy to give to others.

Pretend you are a King or a Queen for a day, and imagine what it would be like to rule a kingdom. Highly regarded spiritual people are also governors of sorts, the Pope, the Dalai Lama, Archbishop Tutu, these are all people who many around the world look to for guidance on spiritual matters. That is a lot of responsibility.

Authors of spiritual books, or singer/songwriters of spiritual songs, have a certain amount of ethics they owe their audience. Being a professional psychic is another form of being looked up to for advice and wisdom. When you work as a spiritual counselor professionally, there is sacred trust you build with your clients. And it is important to replenish. While you may be in a position of authority or leadership, use it wisely, this applies if you manage a business. Ask Haniel to help you be a compassionate leader with a lot of wisdom.

Archangel Haniel:

Aura opal and deep magenta
Sound E Major RAM
Gland Pancreas, digestive system
Crystals citrine,
Essential oils lotus, jasmine, honey suckle, pink roses, rose, white roses, gardenia
Chakra solar plexus chakra,
Key word love, compassion, personal power
Symbol moon, rose, ankh, Venus sign

Angels she supervises from the seventy-two angels:

Vehuel
Daniel
Hahasiah
Imamiah
Nanael
Nitael
Mebahiah
Poyel
Tarot cards she is associated with
The number seven in numerology, seven is the seeker, searcher for truth, and looking for hidden meanings
Seven of wands – your hard work is paying off, keep persevering
Seven of pentacles - taking a rest, return on investments, abundance from hard work
Seven of swords – deception and betrayal, someone is lying about you
Seven of cups – dreams, deception, determination, imagination, having choice about which future to take
The Tower – everything falls apart like an earthquake
The hanged man – indecision, or seeing things from a different point of view

Temperance – balance, this is always an angel card in the traditional tarot

Justice – getting justice legally, or through the law of karma

Angel workout:

"Dear Archangel Haniel, I invite you to embody me. I ask to carry your energy into the world today. I ask you to align my energy with yours. May I be a divine conduit of victory and leadership. Help me speak my truth and see myself clearly. May I radiate divine victory and courage from my solar plexus and think it and speak it throughout the day."

Please help me with:

_____
_____
_____
_____
_____
_____

Please activate my dreams of _____

And protect me always with divine love and divine light

May your energy of love, victory and leadership help me with:

I ask for the highest outcome of all involved

And so it is

Amen

Thank you, Archangel Haniel"

Write about your experiences with Archangel Haniel below:

DAY TWENTY-EIGHT.
ARCHANGEL RAPHAEL

To bring Archangel Raphael to you chant RA FAY EL three times.

Archangel Raphael is the archangel of divine healing.

He oversees healing on a physical level, so call on him anytime you get sick or injured, or if you work in a healing profession of any kind.

Raphael rules the solar plexus chakra along with Archangel Haniel. Haniel brings divine love to the healing and Raphael assists your body with the healing process.

Archangel Raphael name means "god heals" or 'divine healing".

Raphael always shows up with a deep green aura whenever I work with him. But in the aura soma system, he is shown as having a deep blue aura.

The Solar Plexus Chakra

This is the area located in your upper tummy region, located about six inches above your belly button. There is a spinning wheel of beautiful yellow energy. The solar plexus is your place of power. Personal power and power in the world. We each have infinite supply of energy for our spiritual bodies, but a limited supply of life force energy and vitality to use each day. It is essential to take note of where you invest your time, energy, emotions, and note too where your thoughts go. What kinds of thoughts are you having? Where does your mental energy go? And where does your psychic energy go throughout the day?

When I did psychic readings and life coaching professionally fulltime for a decade, a lot of my psychic energy was invested in my clients and helping them. It also went to friends who would show up asking for psychic advice. And to my children. I was last on the list. For a decade I was on auto-pilot, raising teenagers, being a single mom and dealing with other things on a personal level.

After a decade, I got thoroughly exhausted, burned out and collapsed. I was also diagnosed with complex post-traumatic stress too. I had empathy fatigue big time. I went to New Zealand to heal. When I got there the angels said healing would take eighteen months. The first nine months was cocooning. They showed me a picture of a caterpillar in a chrysalis, and said I was to "cocoon" for nine months. The next nine months would be healing, growing and learning until I was out of the post-traumatic stress fog. When a caterpillar is in the cocooning process, it must break its bones over and over to strengthen them, until one day their bones are strong enough to break out of the chrysalis and fly free as a butterfly.

This is literally what happened to me. I broke three bones in my ankle during the second nine months. I didn't know at the time I would literally break bones to become stronger. That was not part of my life plan! Having surgery with my foot being cut open, and plates and screws put in to stabilize my ankle, was *excruciatingly* painful. It is the most painful thing I have ever experienced.

My healing plan involved a lot of getting my personal power back, resting, and having intense therapy with a skilled trauma therapist whose energy was very much like Haniel, gentle, loving and wise. Replenishing my limbic system, adrenal system and restoring my nervous system was crucial.

Archangel Raphael oversaw the physical healing, what kinds of food I was eating, where my energy was going. My nervous system was shot, I had empathy fatigue and adrenal fatigue, along with trauma healing work to do. Healing took eighteen months to get to a point where I could work again. Being in a situation where your health is on the line physically and mentally is scary, because when you first get sick, are in a car accident or injured, or have been diagnosed with a chronic or "life-threatening" disease, it can make you panic. Especially when you don't know the timeline of healing. The thought of maybe never being able to work again, and make money, can be terrifying.

My healing involved eating a plant-based diet, activating my parasympathetic system and calming my central nervous system, getting vitamin B shots, doing yoga, and what really fast-tracked the healing process was doing fifteen minutes of self-hypnosis three times a day, playing alpha music from YouTube.

I like the alpha music that Yellow Brick Cinema has on its YouTube channel, so check it out. I had to learn how to walk again, which was interesting, because a decade earlier I'd had surgery for a burst appendix that poisoned my entire body, and I was in hospital for a month. I had to learn to walk again that year too.

In 2006 I walked away from a marriage, and the next decade was tough. In November of 2016, I was learning to walk again too. This time I was walking towards a new life, and resuming my career as a writer and speaker.

Archangel Raphael rules:

Eight In numerology eight is associated with business skills, leadership and stability

Eight of swords in the tarot – feeling bound or trapped especially mentally, close your eyes, go within, follow inner guidance to break free

Eight of pentacles – perseverance, knowledge, step by step work towards your dreams

Eight of cups – moving on, walking away from emotional baggage or relationship, solitude

Eight of wands – everything is lined up for victory and success

Ten of pentacles -prosperity, wealth, love, happiness

Page of swords, the hermit and the wheel of fortune

The angels from the seventy-two angels who Raphael supervises are:

- Nemamiah
- Yeialel
- Harahel
- Mitzrael
- Umabel
- Iahel
- Anauel
- Mehiel

Gland: Pancreas

Chakra: Solar Plexus (along with Haniel)

Raphael's colors are green, deep blue and yellow. Raphael often shows up with huge golden wings. He is famous for his glory and splendor. He rules the left leg, whereas Haniel, his sister angel rules the right leg. The left side of your body is receptive, and the right side is active. We receive energy on the left side and broadcast it from the right. That is if you are right-handed; if not, your dominant hand is the side that broadcasts energy, and your non-dominant hand is the side of your body where you will receive energy.

Ambidextrous? Use your intuition depending on the situation, and decide in the moment which hand you want to broadcast energy from, and which side you want to receive it.

Raphael will always help you heal.

His crystals are: gold, citrine, jade, greenstone, deep blue sapphire.

He will bring strength to your digestive system. If you are trying to lose weight or stop smoking, call on Raphael for help. Raphael's name means "God heals" or "divine healing".

Angel workout

"Dear Archangel Raphael, I invite you to embody me, Raphael, Raphael, Raphael, May I carry your energy into the world today. I ask you to align my energy with yours. Please strengthen and heal and revitalize every cell in my body. May I be a conduit of divine healing today.

Archangel Raphael help me with:

_____

_____

_____

_____

_____

Please activate my dreams of:

And protect me with divine love and divine light

May your divine energy of healing (add your own request here):

I ask for the highest outcome for all involved

And so it is

Amen

Thank you, Archangel Raphael

Write about your own experience with Archangel Raphael, and remember, you can call on him for healing of any kind. He is like the great physician. Your body has a remarkable ability to heal itself. We can use different tools to help our bodies heal via doctors, surgery, reiki or natural therapies; but the body has the most amazing healing capabilities ever. Thank you, Archangel Raphael. Thank you for your gift of healing.

DAY TWENTY-NINE.
ARCHANGEL GABRIEL

To bring Archangel Gabriel's energy close to you simply chant GAY BREE EL three times

You are sending a phonetic imprint out into the spiritual multiverse to be received and sent back to you. Gabriel will show up immediately.

Gabriel rules the belly chakra, the abdomen and the genitals. She is another Archangel who rules one spinning chakra of light alone; just like Michael does in the heart chakra.

If you are having any problems with pregnancy with sexuality or creativity, call on Gabriel for help. Her energy is loving and kind, and she is one of my dearly beloved Archangels. She told Mary in the Bible that she was pregnant with Jesus, and she rules the Judgement card in the tarot. Known as The Wise Judgement traditionally this card is depicted with Gabriel highly colorized, and the humans underneath her calling out for help as being shadowy. This symbolizes that the spiritual angelic realms are greater than our human ones.

Sometime people ask me: "isn't Gabriel a male angel?" Originally, in Catholic tradition, she was. But during the Middle Ages the Catholic Church gave her a sex change at one of the Vatican councils. Angels are genderless. They just carry a lot of receptive, yin, feminine energy or active, yang, projective masculine energy. This has nothing to do with our human concept of gender. LGBTQ community, please adapt for what works for you.

Gabriel "God is my strength" is an angel who typically serves as a messenger sent from God or divine power to certain people. She is the communicator angel, the patron of musicians, artists and writers.

She also helps the third eye or brow chakra with telepathy. This is because she is so good at helping humans with angelic conversation, delivering messages, networking and helping artists and musicians and writers. Gabriel loves to communicate and plays the trumpet.

It makes sense Gabriel would rule the sacral chakra, because that is where we birth our dreams and desires, as well as physical children. Call on Gabriel for help with any business plan, any artistic desire, any dreams and visions you want to manifest into the physical realm. She will help you. I promise. She has been helping me for years.

Gabriel is the go-to angel for all psychic communication, for all spiritual work, for writing, for networking, for finding the perfect places to speak and teach.

She has always helped me with my writing, with spiritual counselling sessions, with telepathy, visions, insight and mental acuity. She helps me locate lost items. Gabriel is one of my favorite archangels. She is also a good angel to call on for dating advice, psychic dreams, help with pregnancy and help with seeing angels. She is the archangel who will help you birth your dreams and desires into the physical plane. Bringing them from the world of vision and ideas and imagination into tangible form.

Color: archangel Gabriel often shows up to me as indigo blue the color of the brow chakra or third eye. In the aura soma system, she is shown as having a beautiful magenta gold aura.

Gland: spleen, blood sugar, ovaries, urinary tract, adrenals, womb, kidneys

Angels she supervises:

Damabiah
Manakel
Eyael
Habuiah
Reohael
Yabamiah
Hayayel
Mumiah

Tarot cards

The devil (helping with addictions or fears along with archangel Michael)
Nine of cups – contentment, the "wish" card
Nine of wands – rest after hard work
Nine of swords - nightmares
Nine of pentacles – financial security, wealth, luxury
Nine in numerology is generosity, a natural leader
Strength, Judgement, Temperance, high priestess
She is close to the high priestess in the tarot who shows a striking similarity to Mary

Whenever I begin any kind of psychic work, I always begin by asking *"Dear Gabriel, may the information that will best help me and _____ come through in a clear and specific manner. May I be a clear and open channel for divine guidance and divine messages, for the highest good of all. And so it is. Amen."*

That is also the prayer I use as I begin each writing session.

Gabriel's aura can be pink and sparkly as well as blue. She is the archangel who rules the west and emotions.

Archangel Gabriel's name means: God is strong or Divine strength.

Keyword: intuition

Call upon Archangel Gabriel for help with strengthening your intuition.

She can help you by sharpening your intuition and make you more telepathic, receptive, and tender-hearted. In my experience, Gabriel is always kind and loving and has very feminine energy. Maybe because she teaches us how to be receptive and yin energy (feminine energy) is receptive by nature.

Gabriel is the best angel for mothers and musicians and communicators to call on.

Sound YAM

Angel Workout

"Dear Archangel Gabriel, I invite you to embody me. That I may carry your energy into the world today. I ask you to align my energy with yours. May I be a conduit of your angelic energy of divine_____. And radiate divine_____ to all people, places and _____ (specific request)

Please activate my dreams of_____ (specific request)

And protect me with divine love and divine light.

May your divine energy of _____ (add your own request and prayers here)

I ask for the highest and best outcome for all involved. This or something better. And so it is. Amen."

Thank you, Archangel Gabriel"

Write about how Archangel Gabriel has helped you or what she could help you with:

DAY THIRTY. ARCHANGEL URIEL

To bring Archangel Uriel to you chant YOU RAY EL three times

There is some discussion as to whether Uriel and Sandalphon rule the tenth spinning wheel on the Tree of Life, or whether Metatron does. I believe all three of them add their energy to the tenthth wheel. Today, we are going to cover Uriel, and touch on Sandalphon. Uriel also rules the sacral chakra the seat being grounded. Sandalphon is her sister/brother archangel who helps her.

Uriel is one of the four great archangels of the directions. Raphael rules the east, air, spring, swords and the rising sun. Michael rules the south, fire, wands, summer and the midday sun. Gabriel rules the west, water, cups, fall and twilight; and Uriel rules the north, winter, pentacles and midnight.

Uriel means god is my light or divine light. He will help you to manifest things on a day-to-day basis. So, will Sandalphon. They are both archangels of creation and birth.

We all have individual relationships with each archangel, and Uriel's aura is Gold and blue, while Sandalphon's aura is lilac and pale orange. The gold and orange colors blend well for the sacral chakra.

Sandalphon is another large archangel like Metatron. He works on healing your life, and helping you to let go of past losses, grief and sadness; whereas Uriel is a blazing creator archangel to help you set fire to your dreams and passions. Uriel will give you the energy to carry out your plans and projects, and help you birth them into physical form. These two archangels do not have any of the seventy-two angels to supervise. They do have many other angels at their command and they work closely with your guardian angels too.

One thing Uriel is very good at is when you want to send a telepathic message to another person. Ask Uriel to help you talk to that person's guardian angel.

Before you go to sleep at night ask: *"Dear archangel Uriel, I ask that you help me talk to_____. Please ask my guardian angel and _____'s (name of a person you want to send a message to) guardian angel to help with our mental conversation. May all things I say be said with divine light. Please bless my dreams as I sleep, and give me the information that will best help me at this time, and so it is. Amen. Thank you, Archangel Uriel."*

Start your day with an angel prayer and end your day with an angel prayer.Talk continuously with your guardian angel and any archangels or other angels you may be working with too. Angels love you and they want to help you all day long. That is what they are created for. To help humans live more spiritual lives and to bring more of heaven down here on earth. They are the bridge or doorway to the celestial realms.

Uriel can bring you warmth, energy, vitality and strengthen your intuition. Sandalphon will transform and heal your life with divine love. Sandalphon is good at helping people find their soulmates and twin flames.

Uriel is Christ-consciousness, and his symbols are the sun and fire. He will bring you success, and help you transform your life. You can ask Uriel also to set your palms on fire with divine light when you have pain, and want to do some energy healing. Ask Uriel to work through you if want to do laying-on of hands or reiki for yourself or someone else.

Uriel will help you have faith in your potential, and increase your inner sunlight and sense of joy. Uriel says he can help uplift everyone's spirits, ensure success and help you become more charismatic and increase your influence over other people. Not to persuade them to your way of thinking, but rather help you communicate ideas and visions in a way that assures success. Uriel is the success Angel. If you want to be a bright shining star, to have a career as a rock star, a performing artist, or any other kind of star, ask Uriel for help.

The sacral chakra is about giving birth, the belly chakra is the place new life starts and gestates.

Uriel will help you make your ideas and dreams real.

What things do you like to create? How can you bring more creativity into your life?

Almost anything can be creative. Cooking, writing, knitting, graphic design, business plans, getting dressed, being creative is not limited to the creative or performing arts, but also to how you live your life from everything to the way you make love, to the way you cook, and what you bring to every task you perform. Your creativity is unique to you, just as your spiritual DNA and guardian angel are unique to you. No one can create the way that you can, so never be afraid to create. There is no one else on the planet who can create what you can.

You can nourish your creativity by doing things like going to inspiring movies, taking walks in the forest or along the beach, or in a beautiful rose garden, or visiting an art gallery. Even drawing the Flower of Life from scratch and coloring it in can be a form of creativity, as can writing a business plan. Just start somewhere, know that you must let yourself get messy, and not judge the work as you are creating.

Brainstorming, first drafts, or laying the foundation for a piece of art usually require messy work. Then you edit, or re-formulate to get the piece of work the way you want it.

What creative project have you been procrastinating on?

How could you bring more creativity into your life?

What things do you like to create?

How do you express your creativity?

How do you express your creativity, your spirituality and your sexuality? To me, these three are always entwined.

The sacral chakra

Color Red
Sound C major
Gland reproductive system, sexuality, lower back
Chakra: sacral chakra
The sacral chakra is the seat of things you want to give birth to, both literally and metaphorically.

Uriel's name means light of God or divine light. He is the angel who brings us knowledge and understanding of the divine. He is the most sharp-sighted of all the angels. Think of him as the angel of action and clear vision. He will help you develop clarity in your personal life, and with situations and people around you.

Uriel warned Noah about the flood in the Bible, he swooped down to the Garden of Eden on a sunbeam, and stood at the gate with a fiery sword. He is the archangel of natural phenomena like tsunamis, earthquakes, hurricanes, tornados, thunder and storms. Whenever a personal crisis hits your life, Uriel is the archangel to call on. He brings divine retribution and understanding.

Uriel is the archangel who helps us understand why things are the way they are. He carries the flame of knowledge and creation in his hand. Call on him to help you trust in the divine plan of goodness for your life, even when things fall apart. He will show you ultimately how all things lead to your highest good and joy. He will help you interpret your inner voice and dreams, and encourage you to take action. Both Sandalphon and Uriel will work closely with your guardian angel to bring your dreams and plans into fruition.

Angel workout

Invocation

"Dear Archangel Uriel. I invite you to embody me. That I may carry your energy into the world today. I ask you to align my energy with yours. May I be a conduit of your angelic energy of divine_____. And radiate divine_____ to all people, places and _____(specific request)

Please activate my dreams of_____(specific request)

And protect me with divine love and divine light.

May your divine energy of _____(add your own request and prayers here)

I ask for the highest most benevolent outcome

Thank you, Archangel Uriel"

What would you most like Uriel to help you with?

What would you like Uriel to help you manifest?

Write about your experience of Uriel (and Sandalphon too if you want)

Meditate on the images provided of the caddeus and the tree of life, these all represent Jacob's ladder, kundalini energy, a lightning bolt and journeying up and down the stages of the tree. Images provided by copyright free google images.

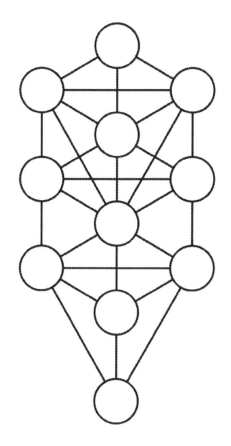

DAY THIRTY-ONE. REVIEWING YOUR PROGRESS

Now you have spent a month talking with your angels every day. I am so proud of you. You get to graduate in angel communication daily home study course. For today, I want to talk about how far you have come, and how much has changed. Where do you still feel blocked and how can you continue your progress?

The angel language is a pictorial and metaphoric language. You communicate with mental pictures, insights, visions and dreams. It is a sensing language; you sense with your five physical senses of taste, touch, hearing, sight and sound. You see repeated number sequences. You close your eyes and spend fifteen minutes in meditation and tune in to the messages your angels have for you. It is very much a two-way conversation:

Prayer, petitions and requests and questions are our messages out to the angels

Meditation, dreams, bodily sensations, synchronicities, gut feelings, and inner knowing are all ways the angels send messages back to us.

It is important with any skill you want to be good at that you practice every day. Spirituality has always been the most important aspect of my life. As a child, I spent hours at Sunday School, as a teenager I was an altar girl, and started a youth group for middle- schoolers. Throughout my adult life, I have studied many different spiritual practices. Ancient history, religions, cultures and customs are a passion of mine. You may have many different passions and hobbies, cultural and spiritual beliefs, but one thing we do share is a love of angels and the desire to have as much angelic help and guidance in our lives as possible.

In my thirty's, I loved Reverend Patrick Pollard, who was the minister at the Center for Spiritual Living in Albuquerque. He inspired me by how devout he was, and how much conviction he lived his life by. I aspired to be like him. I asked him how I could become more spiritual like him. He told me he spent at least two hours a day practicing, whether that was reading, researching, praying, meditating, or whatever spiritual tool he used.

Sometimes we think great spiritual leaders are born that way. Some are. Sometimes we tend to put authors or motivational speakers or spiritual counsellors on a pedestal. Sometimes we put psychics or channels on a pedestal too. What I know is, some people are born with greater psychic ability, but everyone has intuition, and everyone can learn to use their psychic senses. Like any skill, it takes time, daily practice and perseverance. All people face life struggles and a great spiritual leader, a psychic or a doctor, are human just like you and me. So, take the information you like from them, and make it your own. Know we all have our flaws.

The angel language is a subtle language. You use your physical senses to stay grounded, and pay attention. Then you use your intuitive faculties to tune in to divine guidance. There is balance and fine-tuning in learning to be able to walk between both worlds. I hope you continue your angel journey. I hope you have enjoyed getting to know your guardian angel and the other angels presented in this book. I hope you use this book over and over, and learn the techniques and tweak them to make them yours.

But most importantly, I hope you continue to put in twenty minutes a day, at the same time each day, to continue your conversations with your guardian angel. I hope today you will buy another notebook and title it "Conversations with My Guardian Angel" and continue learning how to talk to your angels, and follow the guidance you are given. I hope you have a long, lasting, close relationship with your angels that enriches your life and leaves you feeling guided, supported, loved and comforted always.

Angels are all around you. They love you and want to help you. Their only requirement is that you ask.

We start again where we began:

What one thing would you like your guardian angel to help you with today?

INDEX

Printed in the United States
By Bookmasters